THE CAT IN THE BAG

THE CAT IN THE BAG

The Democratic Party's Assault on America

Howard Towt

EKOT

INTRODUCTION

I am a Republican.

I guess you'd have to say, "A Republican with an Independent streak". I registered as a Republican while I was in college, and did so mostly because I came from a family of Republicans. I grew up on a farm in Oregon, and my mother and her parents were Republicans. I didn't have a compelling reason to join one party or the other. I just wanted to vote in the upcoming election.

I have a mixed presidential voting experience. I voted for Nixon, Reagan, and Bush, but also voted for Carter, Perot, and Clinton. I can't explain the lack of political consistency, other than to say I try to vote for the person I think will do the best job.

I am married to a Democrat. We met in college in the late 1960s. Her parents were Democrats and she is a Democrat. She is a beautiful person, and I love her.

My interest in politics stems from a fascination with the way people behave in a political atmosphere. I've seen instances where people maintain that their principles drive them in a particular direction, but when they vote, issue a verdict, or otherwise commit to the principle, they abandon it and react in a political fashion. It's what makes human beings interesting. To a degree, we are all unpredictable.

But that doesn't mean the subject isn't worth studying. Pollsters attempt to predict elections. Attorneys attempt to figure out what makes prospective jurors "tick". The risks and rewards are high. This is interesting stuff!

This book is a story about American politics. It is my story, and while it raises issues that are important to me, my hope is that it will strike interest in others as well. If nothing else, maybe it will start up a discussion! That can't hurt.

TABLE OF CONTENTS

1

THE REALIZATION

For me, it was during the run-up to the 2004 Presidential Election.

My wife and I enjoy a weekend television program hosted by Charles Osgood that is titled "CBS News Sunday Morning". It has a magazine format that includes political commentary on current events, but also some humor, human interest stories, and in-depth studies of people and places in America. It's worth watching.

The contributors may not be familiar to you. Bill Geist does the "road show" segment of the program. He travels the country spotlighting the unusual and quaint. He brings a "David Letterman" feel to the show, in that his segments are a bit zany. One week you get to see a museum dedicated to tow trucks. Another week it's a watermelon seed-spitting contest. It's good fun.

The political commentary features Nancy Giles and Ben Stein. Their presentations are entertaining and enlightening, and sometimes quite poignant.

The one part of the show that we try not to miss is the ending segment. The program closes with footage of wildlife in various parts of the United States. It might be Sandhill Cranes in the Bosque del Apache or Bighorn Mountain Sheep in Colorado. Seasonal changes are highlighted, and it's all done without background music. The audio is simply the natural sounds of the location being filmed. It makes you feel good to be in America.

One of the programs in 2004 included a look at environmental policy in the United States. It had an interview with Secretary of the Interior Gale Norton on a picnic bench in a National Park setting. She talked about balancing the needs of the public with the need to preserve the natural beauty of our parks. My overall impression was that it was a pretty good statement of the mission of the Department of the Interior, and it highlighted current challenges faced by the Department.

The program then switched to an opposing view of the subject.

The images shown were not of the opposing speaker, but of the problems associated with an environmental policy run amok. I remember hearing an off-screen voice talking about President Bush being the worst environmental president in United States history; that President Bush was personally destroying our American outdoors. Startling images were presented: the smoldering aftermath of a forest fire; logging equipment clear-cutting a forest; fish dying in a stream.

My wife was watching the program along with me. At the conclusion, I asked what she thought of the story, and was amazed at her answer. She thought it was a fair depiction of both sides of the issue.

I was stunned! What I had seen was an ambush. Secretary Norton had presented a rundown of current policy statements on the environment. The opposing view was inflammatory rhetoric making stinging accusations and personal attacks. It didn't seem balanced to me at all.

The moderator didn't follow up the "worst environmental president" accusation with any questions such as, "Who is the second worst, and who is the best". Or, "What scale of measurement did you use to determine your rankings?" The accusations were unchallenged. They were accepted as fact.

I kept trying to understand what was going on with the segment. It was jarring. The rest of the program had followed the standard "Sunday Morning" format, yet this piece was extreme.

The forest fire images seemed familiar to me. I think they came from an earlier news piece that had shown damage from forest fires during the 2003 drought in the Western United States. My recollection was that the complete footage showed fire damage to an area that had not been thinned, and then panned to an area that had been thinned. The intent of the film had been to show that forests thinned of underbrush were less likely to be catastrophically hurt by forest fires. President Bush was pushing a forest thinning initiative at the time.

The dead fish footage also seemed familiar. I think it came from a story about Oregon farmers needing water for their land during the drought. The issue was that if water was taken from the river, fish would die, but that if the water wasn't provided to the farmers, they faced financial ruin. It pointed out the difficult decisions that have to be made during times of drought.

The logging operations footage didn't trigger any recent memories. However, it certainly left an impression of land being destroyed for the purpose of obtaining lumber.

I hate to say I'm obsessed by this particular segment within a "CBS News Sunday Morning" program, but it bothered me on several levels:

--Why did it appear so slanted to me, and yet my wife thought it was balanced?

--Why was it deemed appropriate for the "CBS News Sunday Morning" format?

--What was the intent of CBS?

It started me thinking about the packaging of our television programming. I had heard stories of bias in the news, but hadn't paid much attention to them. Was there something to them? Is there an agenda at play here?

I began to take notes.

2

ESTABLISHMENT IDEOLOGY

Before we get too much further into this book, I should probably define myself in a bit more detail. I realize we are all biased in one way or another, so let me explain the things that make up my biases.

I am a white male. I haven't researched my ethnicity, but imagine I am descended from Western European immigrants.

I come from a "broken home". My parents divorced before I entered grade school. I was raised by my mother and my grandparents.

I am a veteran. I was a pilot during the Vietnam War, flying the F-105G Thunderchief. I was based in Thailand, and flew missions over Vietnam and Cambodia during 1972 and 1973.

I am a product of public education in the United States. I attended public schools in Oregon and California, was a freshman at the University of California in Berkeley (Go Bears!), and graduated from the USAF Academy in Colorado. I attended graduate school at Purdue University (MS in Engineering) and got an MBA from Denver University. American taxpayers paid for most of my education, including my use of the GI Bill to attend DU.

My religious background is a bit muddy. I started out as a Presbyterian, but ended up a member of The Federated Church when we moved to a small town in Northern California (Crescent City). I think the town was not big enough to support both a Presbyterian and a Methodist constituency, so the two denominations joined forces as The Federated Church.

I married my wife in a Catholic ceremony, and have attended Catholic services with her since then. While I would technically classify my religion as "Protestant", I have to say that I am not a religious person. I did not receive the "gift of faith".

With that being said, I hope I have not alienated anyone. Like each of you, I consider myself to be a "normal person". I am a work in progress, and am thankful to be able to enjoy the life experience.

But back to the story...

The year 2004 was an awakening for me. After that "CBS News Sunday Morning" episode I watched earlier, I was a changed man. Rather than simply listen to the news, I began to look for patterns and themes in the presentation. I had always assumed that our news organizations were dedicated to providing information and understanding, and to a great extent that is true. However, the "understanding" part of the mission is where things get sticky. One can be given information, but based on the techniques used in the presentation of that information, you can understand it in dramatically different ways.

Probably the most obvious example is in the coverage of the Middle East. Like most of you, prior to 2001 I had never heard of Al Jazeera. Although it is an established news network, it doesn't disseminate much of its information in English, and all of us with Basic Cable TV service didn't find it included in our list of channels.

All that changed after the United States began military operations in Afghanistan. We were treated to mob scenes of people showing their hatred for the United States. Often, the footage would be courtesy of the Al Jazeera network. It seemed that while the United States thought it was doing good things, the depiction through the lens of an Al Jazeera cameraman was something different.

I can remember news programs where commentators would try to explain the reason that the coverage by Al Jazeera took on such a different tone from the coverage of the other news services. The common perception was that the coverage was simply "cultural". We in the United States expect a certain point of view, while people in the Middle East expect a different point of view. News networks (including Al Jazeera) simply reflect their respective dominant cultures.

I could accept that. I didn't like that Al Jazeera was fanning anti-American sentiment, but if that's what they had to do to stay in business, so be it. What was more interesting was that what I considered to be "anti-American sentiment" was perceived as the cultural norm by Al Jazeera. The right thing for them to do was to lace anti-American themes throughout their coverage.

When military operations began in Iraq, Al Jazeera stayed true to form. They embellished their coverage with footage of actual combat operations, this time showing images of urban fighters shooting at the enemy. The unspoken message of the images was that the enemy was the American soldier.

That theme seemed to be picked up by the BBC. During the fighting leading up to the fall of Baghdad, the BBC coverage depicted the American effort as being flawed, while the Iraqi resistance was depicted as being confident and determined. I can remember being frustrated by the coverage from the reporters embedded with U. S. forces that simply showed military vehicles moving through the desert. Their reports confirmed that military operations were being conducted, but the BBC reports provided context and theme: Americans were milling around in sandstorms while Baghdad was secure and confident.

I did a lot of channel-surfing, trying to get the full story. The coverage of Iraq was different depending on what channel you were watching. I gradually lost loyalty to any single network. I began to see differences in not only network coverage, but in the individuals reporting the news. Analysts had different perspectives, depending on their backgrounds. I began to choose favorites. I really liked Col. David Hunt. His gravelly voice and shoot-from-the-hip responses were refreshing. He exuded credibility and honesty.

Let me pause for a moment and summarize some thoughts. I grew up using newspapers and newsmagazines as sources for school reports. It never occurred to me that the reports might not be accurate. Similarly, the Six O'Clock News on television seemed to be an unimpeachable source. It provided a summarization of the events of the day, letting us know what was important in the world.

I was attracted to a news program based upon the style of the commentator or upon a signature segment that was fun. (Think in terms of Andy Rooney on "60 Minutes".) The information presented was simply that: information. What I didn't realize was that there was a theme associated with the information. There was a specific way in which the events of the day were being represented. That was the "substance" of the newscast. As long as the theme fit with my cultural perspective, I didn't notice it. I could even be moved out of my comfortable space with an occasional jarring news message as long as it was temporary and not too frequent. Life was good!

But I have to say our American military involvement in the Middle East caused me to re-think my perceptions. Here were daily examples of people who hated me because I was born in America. Places of worship were being used to store weapons, and that was OK. Hospitals and schools were being used as fortresses, and nobody took exception. People were using beheadings and summary execution to make political points, and they were classified as freedom-fighters or "The Resistance". All of a sudden, things going on in that part of the world were on the front page of the newspapers. Anti-Americanism was the cultural norm.

And what about the suicide attacks? This was a most difficult concept to understand. I like to think of these things as an aberration, but there was a whole culture that glorified them. Should that culture be celebrated for its diversity? What if that culture is dedicated to the proposition of destroying MY life? Must I be tolerant of such a culture?

Regardless of how I felt, there were a lot of people with

a strong anti-American bias. I know it's not everyone in the Middle East (Israelis being the most obvious exception), but the programs presented by Arabian TV certainly conveyed the impression that the cultural norm was to hate Americans. One felt comfortable if that was the way you felt. Others with whom you associated were anti-American, and even if you didn't know them, you assumed they felt a hatred for America. Hating Americans was simply the expected thing to do. These were not abstract notions. Americans were being killed by people bent on performing individual acts of suicide to show their religious faith; people would strap on an explosive vest with the same sense of reverie as others might take communion. It was a jarring mindset to behold.

But if anti-American culture is the norm in the Middle East, what would be our norm in North America? Is there a dominant ideological culture here? What is The Establishment teaching us?

This is where things start to get interesting.

In North America, the dominant culture is anti-Republican.

3
ABSTRACTIONS & CODE WORDS

"What did he just say? What kind of a right-wing zealot is this guy?"

I can feel the backlash coming…

"You can't criticize The Establishment. It is what we are! It is our culture!"

I've got to ask you to suspend reality for just a moment and assume that what I say is true: We have an anti-Republican culture. Given that assumption, how does one benchmark it? What are the guideposts? Is it just as difficult to point out anti-Republican culture in America as it is to point out anti-American culture in the Middle East? Remember, if you are living the culture, you don't see the bias.

I think we have to look at this phenomenon from the standpoint of a melodrama. I am being literal here. I don't know if you've ever been to a melodrama, but it is a play where the good guys and the bad guys are easily distinguishable. If the audience needs to be warmed up, the actors come out before the play and introduce themselves and demonstrate the appropriate reactions to take when they appear during the performance. The person in the black hat with the long mustache and sinister expression is the bad guy. Whenever he appears, he is to be greeted with hisses and boos. The person in the white hat with the blindingly bright smile is the good guy, and he is to be greeted with cheers, shouts of encouragement and general acclamation. You get to practice as the actors alternately appear and encourage you to exhibit the appropriate response. It is true audience interaction and it is fun!

Think of a melodrama when you see the evening news. Watch for the anti-Republican signs. For example, Republican figures are typically depicted as being "under siege". If the American President happens to be a Republican, watch for the news coverage of whatever public event he or she is attending to also include a segment of a protest group nearby, carrying signs indicating that the President is a bad person in some way. The impression to convey is that no matter what the event, the President's appearance is an affront and an outrage to concerned Americans. We see it as natural and right that Republican political figures are harassed at any public events they attend. The protests are a natural occurrence in our culture; just as natural as rain on a parade. Watch for the opposite coverage of a Democratic Party event. The people there are definitely NOT "under siege". They are cast as mainstream, informed, and caring.

At the risk of beating a dead horse, also watch for blame being placed after a disastrous event of some type. It can be on foreign shores or American shores. It can be natural or man-made. It can be big or small. The important part is the first few reports to be broadcast. They will place blame somewhere, and it will invariably fall on the shoulders of Republicans.

Be sure to note where the Democrats are located in the chain of responsibility. If the first responders are Republicans and the supervisors are Democrats, the first responders will have their errors highlighted. Conversely, if the first responders are Democrats and the supervisors are Republicans, supervision will be where the major problems occurred. The key is in the timing of the news coverage of the event. The first few reports will highlight the failings of Republicans. As more time passes, the appropriate blame will be assessed and the true breakdowns will be reported.

I think you will be surprised at how often this sequence of reporting takes place. Every time there is an earthquake, a tsunami, or an odd weather phenomenon, you will see the effect. But you will have to watch for it. The point is often made subtly, and the news reporters are not obligated to explain to you the techniques being used.

I'm not asking you to play the part of a detective here; just be an observer. Keep in mind that the melodrama of the reporting will play out in those early reports. As you watch the news segment, ask yourself, "Who is wearing the black hat here?" It will amaze you how often one group in particular is cast as the villain.

But frequently, there will be confusion because of the use of terminology and the images that are shown. Let me shine some light on this.

THE DEMOCRAT PARTY

Sometimes a melodrama will play out with the good guy acting all by himself. However, often the good guy is supported by a team. You might have seen a play or a movie where a town banded together to take back control from a gang of one sort or another. The good guy is in front, but the families in the town stand behind him.

It is time to introduce a special terminology. Please note the spelling of "The Democrat Party" in the heading at the top of the prior paragraph. It is different than the spelling of the Democratic Party. The Democratic Party is a political party, just like the Republican Party. When I use the term "Democrat Party", it denotes the embodiment of Democratic Party ideology. It is an abstraction, and the best way I can explain it is this way: It is the counterpart to "The Vast Right Wing Conspiracy".

The Democrat Party has no membership, other than through a belief system: If you believe in The Vast Right Wing Conspiracy, you are (figuratively speaking) a card-carrying member of the Democrat Party. Another appealing aspect of the Democrat Party is that it doesn't matter what your actual political party affiliation is. You can be unaffiliated, an Independent, or support the Green Party and still be a member of the Democrat Party.

You might wonder, "What drives people to be aligned with the Democrat Party?" The answer is that it promises two very significant benefits to each and every member:

1) The Democrat Party will make you popular.
2) The Democrat Party will get you more than the next guy.

Think back to the third grade in elementary school. These two promises address some very basic needs, and we seek them out. If everyone likes you, and you are doing better than the next person, you are happy. The Democrat Party exists to serve these two instinctive needs.

How does this tie into our anti-Republican culture? It happens that the Democrat Party is the source of this culture in the United States. Think of yourself as landing on foreign soil and having to adapt as quickly as possible. You look around and try to determine what makes up the popular culture. You instinctively know that if you accept the feelings and beliefs of the popular culture, you will fit in. To "fit in" to the American culture, you are strongly encouraged to be anti-Republican. That's the work of the Democrat Party, and it has great appeal to several groups of people. That would include, for example, personalities in the entertainment industry who make their living by being liked. If your career rises and falls based on whether people like you, you will be naturally drawn to the Democrat Party.

If you haven't thrown this book down in disgust by now, I have a couple of examples for you to consider. Michael Moore created a film titled "Fahrenheit 9/11". It is represented as a documentary, and it portrays its main character, President Bush, as a liar, a moron, and a miserable failure. The film won the 2004 Cannes Film Festival award for Best Picture.

I don't know if you saw the movie in a theatre or not, but if you did, you will not be surprised by what I am going to say next. At the conclusion of the film, THE AUDIENCE STOOD AND CLAPPED.

I think this illustrates two points. First, the film resonates with the audience. It speaks "Truth". Second, it establishes Michael Moore as a member of the Democrat Party. He puts on display, for all to see, the emblematic characteristics of Republicans, with President Bush represented as the Republican "Everyman". He shows what irritates so many Americans: The country somehow elected a Republican who exemplifies the traits of his group (stupid, lying, and a failure), and he is still leading our country!

The film is not so much of an attack on an individual as it is a representation of the people classified as Republicans. Imagine yourself being a member of that group and being surrounded by people in a movie theatre who applaud the stereotypical features of that group.

While you are getting your mind around that image, go back later in 2004 to a person named Mary Mapes. She worked for CBS and produced a story on President Bush that was supported by documents that helped enforce the perception of the Republican President being stupid, lying and a miserable failure while he was serving with the Texas Air National Guard. The documents used by Ms. Mapes to illustrate her point were prepared on word-processing equipment that didn't exist at the time the documents were dated. She continues to be amazed that people focus on the issue of the authenticity of the documents. Her point is that the story spoke "Truth", and that the supporting documents are a minor issue. Ms. Mapes is a member of the Democrat Party.

The main point in all of this is that if you live in America, you would do well to align with the Democratic Party, since you will be supported and not attacked. You will be a part of the dominant culture (The Establishment) and thus don't have to go through the painful exercise of defining yourself in terms of issues.

Don't be put off by this cultural phenomenon and its terminology. We need to get our arms around the forces at work here, and understanding the anti-Republican sentiment in the United States is a really helpful way to think about our culture. And remember: if you think there's a Vast Right Wing

Conspiracy out there, you are a member of the Democrat Party.

OK, then. So much for abstractions in our anti-Republican culture. There are certainly more of them, and we'll touch on them in the pages that follow. However, there are also "code words" at work here. These are the words that trip us up when we are trying to communicate with one another. I'll give you three examples to consider

CONSERVATIVE

Here's a word that can be used as a noun or an adjective. Dictionaries describe the adjective form of the word in terms like "favoring traditional values" or "tending to oppose change". You also see descriptive words like "cautious" or "restrained" when looking for synonyms.

The Democratic Party amplifies the dictionary definitions and adds an emotional component. I'll use a capital "C" to highlight the differences.

First, let's note that the Democratic Party uses the term without the capital "C" to refer to members of its own party. I think a good example of this is the late Governor of Alabama and Democratic Party presidential candidate, George Wallace.

Governor Wallace was a political force in the 1960s and 1970s. He was a segregationist in the 1960s and was strongly opposed to the civil rights movement. When you hear the Democratic Party refer to these aspects of his political life, however, he is described as a conservative. I can remember reading one article where it spoke of his segregationist activities, and it never mentioned that he was a Democrat. Rather, he, and other Democrats of his time such as Orvil Faubus (former Governor of Arkansas) and Lester Maddox (former Governor of Georgia) are referred to as conservatives. All of these ex-Governors have pages of history written about their segregationist activities. They were all Democrats at one time, but the Democratic Party does not tend to point out this fact.

Just as an aside, it is of interest to me that Governor Wallace at one time had the endorsement of the NAACP (National Association for the Advancement of Colored People) when he was running for political office. It seems ironic that a political group dedicated to the advancement of people with dark skin color would be aligned with a person who wants to bar them from going to the same bathrooms, going to the same schools, and eating in the same restaurants as people with lighter skin tones. You might wonder, "Where's the principle!" I suppose there could be valid reasons for the logic of the stance, but the point to note here is that the NAACP remains dedicated to the Democratic Party.

Getting back on track, and summarizing a bit, the word "Conservative" can also be used in a disparaging manner. This is the capital "C" version of the word. Someone can say, "You Conservative!" and not actually care about your political stance. Think in terms of someone saying, "You bastard!" You wouldn't necessarily feel the need to point out that you are well acquainted with your father. Rather, you would take it as a disparaging remark, and go on.

While the Democratic Party rarely, if ever, uses the word "Conservative" in a positive context, the use of the word as a pejorative is not its only use. This is when the Democratic Party uses it to broadly denote people who do not consistently spread anti-Republican thought. The columnist George Will provides a good example of how this usage is applied.

Mr. Will is an analyst with a conservative point of view. He writes a syndicated column that appears about once a week, and he writes about varied topics, from economics to politics; international relations to baseball. He is educational in his approach, filling his columns with data that support his points and making us all better informed in the process. The problem from the Democratic Party point of view is that he does not push an anti-Republican ideology.

I'm sure Mr. Will would say he is just commenting on current events, providing historical context, and helping us all understand the goings-on in our world. I'll bet he also thinks he is more of a realist than a political partisan. However, because his remarks are not consistently anti-Republican, he is labeled a Conservative.

But what if you actually try to promote Republican thought? Now you've stepped over the line. Now you are an Ultra-Conservative! It's the difference between being passive and being active. Avoiding anti-Republican rhetoric labels you as a Conservative. Promoting a conservative point of view makes you an Ultra-Conservative.

To sum up, the term "conservative" has emotion attached to it when used by the Democratic Party. If a person does not consistently promote an anti-Republican theme in his or her political statements, the person is a Conservative. If instead one actually advocates pro-Republican themes, he or she is an Ultra-Conservative.

If you happen to be in the news business, you can devote your complete program to regular content, but you must include at least one anti-Republican sentiment somewhere in the program to avoid being labeled a Conservative. If you've got a long history of consistent anti-Republican references in your programming content, you are cut a little slack. You might be able to slip by without anti-Republican sentiment on rare occasions, but you risk being labeled by the Democratic Party.

For comparison, take opinion columnists like Molly Ivins, Maureen Dowd, and Paul Krugman. Check out their writings and note the anti-Republican sentiment. (If you are not accustomed to reading opinion pieces, this is the time to get started.) You will see why these three individuals will never be labeled a Conservative.

DISENFRANCHISE

This word, according to the dictionary, means to deprive of voting rights. That's simple enough, but to the Democrat Party (note that we're dropping the "ic" here), it is much, much more. Disenfranchisement, to the Democrat Party, is the setting apart of a class of individuals who do not have access to basic freedoms and rights. It stands for the anger and frustration of these people. It implies desperation and victimhood. It legitimizes anti-social behavior, and sometimes legitimizes criminal behavior. It is truly much more than being deprived of voting rights.

And here is the kicker: The Democrat Party holds as a core belief that Republicans cause disenfranchisement.

I can remember having a talk with a friend where the subject of voting abnormalities in recent elections came up. I pointed out that there were several allegations made, including that people were disenfranchised because there were too many voters in line, and that other people appeared to have been disenfranchised because too few people showed up to vote. It seemed that no matter what the turnout, the "disenfranchisement" accusation was always made by the Democrat Party, and that there were just no law suits that showed it was a problem.

He stopped me and explained that he was talking about "disenfranchisement" in the larger sense, not just the voting aspect.

At the time, I didn't think much of the comment, other than maybe I needed to consult the dictionary and see if there was a secondary definition of which I was unaware. At some point, I did check the dictionary, and strangely, there was no secondary definition.

What to make of this? Could it be that the dominant culture in America is gradually modifying word usage? I guess that happens, since our language is continually evolving. But what is going on with this particular word?

And then it hit me. The word was in the process of becoming an emotion-laden metaphor, just like "racism". Is it just happening that way of its own accord, or is something driving it? Who could possibly benefit by an expanded definition of the word, "disenfranchisement"? (Maybe you see where I'm going here.)

This is my thought: There has to be a continual renewal of emotionally-charged words to help the Democrat Party keep its grip on those it classifies as victims. If "racism" starts to lose its punch because we see highly-paid, highly visible entertainers and political figures with dark skin color, and it makes less and less sense to grant them and their offspring special privileges, how does one adapt?

How about a new class of victims that are "disenfranchised"? They move to the edges of society, or in some cases, work outside the bounds of society. They are "disenfranchised" because of their religious beliefs or perhaps because they are of a particular cultural heritage. All of a sudden, "disenfranchised" becomes a term for all victims of Republican wrongdoing. It has legs!

I think we can watch for greater and greater usage of the term "disenfranchised". It might even turn out that dictionary definitions will be modified to include the expanded definition. A leading indicator of this trend will be the Reverend Jesse Jackson. After each election, he perceives instances of disenfranchisement by Republicans. As voting becomes more electronic, there will be (despite protestations by the Democrat Party) less and less voter fraud. When voting becomes less problematic, then classical "disenfranchisement" will become less of an issue, and if Reverend Jackson still sees disenfranchisement, it will have to be of the expanded kind. It will be interesting to see how the definition of the word changes over time.

MODERATE

This word is traditionally used as an adjective, meaning "not excessive or extreme". However, when it is used as a noun, it becomes a political term. The idea is that when you are a "Moderate", you don't hold extreme political views.

Let's start off with a poll. The poll includes just two questions:

1. Which political ideology best describes you:
a. Liberal.
b. Moderate.
c. Conservative.

2. Which best describes your stand on the issue of abortion:
a. Pro-Choice, and I expect others to support a woman's right to choose.

b. Pro-Choice, but I accept that others may choose to be Pro-Life.

c. Pro-Life for myself and my immediate family, but I support a woman's right to choose.

d. Pro-Life for myself and my immediate family, and I expect others to be Pro-Life.

My bet is that the distribution of the answers to both questions would look like a "bell curve". In other words, most of the respondents would choose the middle answers. Question 1 would be answered "b", and Question 2 would be answered either "b" or "c". Most people think they are "Moderate" and most people are tolerant of the views of others on the abortion question.

What's the lesson here? It's that the "Moderate" terminology highly correlates with our stand on abortion. If we are rigidly Pro-Life, we are probably a Conservative; if we are rigidly Pro-Choice, we are probably a Liberal. And so I will make a pronouncement:

The terminology "Liberal", "Moderate", or "Conservative" is just a proxy for your stand on abortion. You don't need to divulge your positions on taxation, government regulation, or interpretation of the Constitution. All we need to know is where you stand on abortion.

You might think that this is a pretty sweeping generalization, but here is how I justify it. I'm a "70% of the time" kind of person. That means that if something happens 70% of the time, I take it as a pretty good fact. That doesn't mean it is "Truth"; just that you can count on it.

Why 70%? The logic goes something like this: If I can be right 70% of the time, that means I am wrong 30% of the time. If I'm placing bets with equal probability, over time I net 40% on the deal. If my overhead is half of my revenue, I end up with 20% before taxes, pay about half of the profit in taxes, and end up with a return of 10% for my effort. Anytime you can make a solid 10% return, you probably ought to do it!

Anyway, if I assume that based upon your stance on

abortion I can predict your political ideology and be right 70% of the time, I am happy. It makes me appear to know what I'm talking about!

Here's another takeoff on the abortion issue: To be a member of the Democratic Party, you must be "Pro-Choice". It is like taking an oath of office. If you cannot say that you support "a woman's right to choose", you cannot consider yourself a real Democrat. The way you get around this is to say you are a "Moderate", which is a code word for being a Pro-Life Democrat who accepts others as being Pro-Choice. This is why it is so difficult for members of the Democratic Party to say they are liberal in their ideology. The term "Liberal" is a code word for a rigid belief in abortion rights, both as an individual and for others. This is actually a minority stance in the Democratic Party, so it makes sense that most Democrats consider themselves "Moderates".

Maybe it's time to pause for a moment and see if we can intellectually get our arms around this issue. We are not talking about the Democrat Party here. This is the Democratic Party, and it is defined in terms of a single issue. The genius of the Party is that the issue is wrapped in the imagery of a metaphorical phrase: "A Woman's Right to Choose". It turns abortion into an empowering, enabling concept of choice and individual rights. Without knowing what the phrase embodies, everyone would support it. It would be medieval to say that you think it is right to deny women rights or to deny women choices. The phrase stands on its own as a statement of power and freedom. Thus it has strong imagery and has deep feelings attached to it. It is an incredibly good rallying point.

It also has pathos. If you challenge a female on "A Woman's Right to Choose", you are setting yourself up to receive a lecture on back-alley abortions and "the way things were". There is suffering. There is sorrow. There is release from bondage. This is a unifying issue, and there is no turning back. The blood has been spilt (so to speak): the right to an abortion will not be abridged.

And so it is settled. "A Woman's Right to Choose" is the

rallying cry of the Democratic Party. It defines the Democratic Party.

But what if you choose not to accept this statement as fact? I apply the 70% rule, and say, "That's the way it is." But you still don't believe me, and want to figure out a way to test the assertion.

You decide to test it by polling registered Democrats. Simply ask the question, "Do you believe in abortion?" The responses would be over 70% affirmative, but probably not by much. Phrase the question, "Are you Pro-Choice?" and again, affirmative responses would exceed 70%. But ask the question, "Do you support a woman's right to choose?" and you can expect affirmative responses of close to 100% (within the margin of statistical error). Do an informal poll of your friends who are Democrats. I think you will be amazed at how strong the correlation is between members of a political party and a particular tenet of their beliefs.

I know, I know. You are saying that classifying things by virtue of a 70% or greater probability is simplistic. And I agree. But it sure does help gain an understanding of what's going on in American politics.

Think in terms of a card game like Bridge. You don't need to be an expert to enjoy and understand the game. Take a few lessons or read a basic-level book, and you are off and running. Sophistication will come with time. Just start out by learning a few of the rules of the game and you will enjoy it and appreciate it.

This book is a "starting point". Understand some of the concepts and some of the code words, and you will begin to see the common threads that run through the politics at work in our country. I'm not expecting you to become an overnight pundit, but I am interested to see if you see the same things that I do, particularly in the next chapter.

We'll start with the themes.

4

THEMES OF THE DEMOCRATIC PARTY

What is a theme? It is the message that sticks with you after the event has passed. Did you see the movie "Dr. Zhivago"? Whenever you hear Lara's Theme ("Somewhere, My Love" – composed by Maurice Jarre), do you feel that sense of sorrow; the haunting feeling of love lost? That's what music can do. It can cause you to be overcome by emotion. Images are just as powerful, and words have emotional power as well. The feelings they create can overwhelm you. We are all susceptible to these emotions because we are human beings. But are there powerful themes in the Democratic Party? Let's look at a few examples.

With Hurricane Katrina in 2005, the network news extensively covered the devastation caused by the hurricane. That, at least, was the outward appearance. However, as you watched more and more of the coverage, a theme began to appear. The first indication was in the reports that President Bush delayed the federal response to the tragedy, thereby causing needless deaths. The second indication was in the rumors that National Guard troops had been deployed to bring about security in New Orleans and had been ordered "to shoot to kill". The third indication was when a rap singer named Kanye West was quoted as saying, "George Bush doesn't care about black people".

If you hadn't figured out the theme before that moment, it hit you in the face: REPUBLICANS ARE RACIST! The news reports seemed to dwell on the devastation in New Orleans as living proof of this assertion.

This message was a bit tough to receive. Those of us on the Republican side of things had to take a moment to get over the shock of the accusation.

But how did we know this was a theme? The answer is because it resonated. It had impact. It's what we remember. And it's also where the melodrama takes off. The TV coverage is of people talking about the problems Republicans have with their image. How should the Republicans behave now that their racism is on display? You begin to see the picture painted with the bad people wearing black hats, and those bad people are Republicans.

Normally, the themes of the Democratic Party are more subtle. You see images of devastation followed by an interview with a Democratic Congressperson saying, "Someone has to take the blame for this!" It is left for the viewer to determine who the "someone" is. Hints are given: George Bush, on vacation in Texas, didn't take the tragedy seriously. The city of New Orleans has a large population of poor people who are mostly of dark skin color. Poor people were not given the assistance they needed, and the inference is that Republicans wanted it that way.

Sometimes the themes are just totally off-the-wall. The anti-war efforts of Cindy Sheehan come to mind. This was a movement in the August to September timeframe of 2005 that involved a mother whose son was killed in Iraq. Maybe you could categorize this as just another anti-war protest, but this time there was a difference. Ms. Sheehan was requesting an audience with the President of the United States to help her understand why her son died. Several months earlier she had met with the President, but she was demanding another meeting. This time she wanted to hear "The Truth". The theme of her anti-war cause was never explicitly stated, but her point was abundantly clear: DEMOCRAT BLOOD IS MORE IMPORTANT THAN THE BLOOD OF OTHERS.

I suppose Ms. Sheehan should get credit for distilling the

anti-war message down to a coherent theme for the Democratic Party. This theme is much easier to understand than one trying to get across the point that the Democratic Party supports our troops, except those soldiers who support the Republican Party. Or that the Democratic Party mourns the deaths of our soldiers, even though they died supporting an unjust, immoral, and illegal war.

It is a complicated message, and is actually an "Anti-Military" theme. If you are wondering how a "We support the troops" message becomes an anti-military theme,   consider the Pro-Palestinian message. It is similarly complex, in that it expresses support for the Palestinian people but not their leaders and not their mission (destruction of the Jewish state). Likewise, you might support the troops, but not their leaders (from the President on down) and not their mission (peacekeeping in Iraq). The Pro-Palestinian message is actually an Anti-Israel message. The Pro-Troops message is actually an Anti-Military message.

But this idea of assigning a higher value to Democrat blood is an incendiary theme! It is truly one of the most divisive and partisan messages you can deliver, and it was delivered day-in and day-out for six weeks. It did upset a few people and caused some counter-demonstrations, but the theme was played over and over during the summer of 2005 with the customary "affirmation of silence". That's the characteristic of the anti-Republican culture at work: you are conditioned to expect to hear that Republicans are bad. When Kanye West made his accusation, there was clamoring support from Democratic Congressmen, particularly those with dark skin color. The Kanye West remark was celebrated for its honesty. It appeared that only Laura Bush, the President's wife, was "disgusted" with the comment.

There are two points to note about Mr. West's assertion. First, this kind of anti-Republican sentiment is culturally endorsed (as evidenced by the general lack of outrage to the comment). Second, it is extracted from a list of recurring themes that are replayed day-in and day-out by the Democratic Party.

You say you are not aware of the themes? Let me give you a quick list, and see if they sound familiar. I'll go over each of them in more detail, but right now, here they are, in bullet format:

- Republican are bad people (racist, homophobic, and bigoted).
- Republicans are destroying the environment.
- Republicans are harming our children.
- Republicans are stealing from our Seniors.
- Republicans are shredding the Constitution.
- Republicans are turning the economy into a catastrophe.

There are just six of them, and the first one is a bit of a catch-all. I've found that without too much trouble, they can be memorized. If you can commit them to memory, you won't be surprised when you hear one or more of them covered on any network news program on any given day of the week.

Sometimes they are subtly presented, but often they are punctuated with an exclamation. A commentator or some other public figure will provide the thematic context by explaining how the particular news situation of the day shows Republicans are (pick one or more) bad people, destroying the environment, harming our children, stealing from our Seniors, shredding the Constitution, or turning the economy into a catastrophe. It passes for "analysis", but it is that part of the news that "aids our understanding" and reinforces the anti-Republican culture.

I can see some examples are going to be needed here. We'll go over each of the themes in turn.

REPUBLICANS ARE BAD PEOPLE

I mentioned that the "Bad Republican" theme has three separate components. Let's start with the first component: Republicans are racists. We know that Republicans are cast in the role of wearing the black hats in our cultural melodrama. In that role, Republicans are certainly cast as being mean-spirited, but do they embody racism? Isn't that a bit extreme?

In the classroom, we learn that racism is a human trait; that it arises from our tendency to favor people who are similar to us and stay away from people who are different from us. But does this universality hold true in the political world? Take, for example, an organization dedicated to ending racism. The A.N.S.W.E.R. Coalition (Act Now to Stop War and End Racism) works to build unity against racism. You would think that it would work across party lines within the United States. However, that doesn't seem to be the case. A.N.S.W.E.R. works almost exclusively with factions of the Democratic Party, to the exclusion of the Republican Party. Why is that? Is it because there are no racists in the Democratic Party?

Let's refine that question a bit. I know it's hard to believe, but is it possible that the Democratic Party think racist behavior relates only to Republicans? See if you can get a Democrat to name someone in his or her own party who is a racist. Even with historical figures like Jefferson Davis who took our southern states and seceded from the Union in order to perpetuate slavery, or Governor George Wallace who defied federal intervention to keep schools segregated, you will find that many Democrats won't be able to name a racist member of their own party. Even with Senator Robert Byrd's history of involvement with the Ku Klux Klan, you won't find acknowledgement that a Democrat could be a racist. Within the Democratic Party, there appears to be widespread acceptance of the "fact" that only Republicans are racists.

My favorite example is that of the late Senator Strom Thurmond. He was a Democrat until he was in his sixties, and then switched parties to become a Republican. While he was a Democrat, Senator Thurmond was well respected, and nothing was made of the fact that he fathered a child with a black teenage maid at his family home in South Carolina. However, when he became a Republican, all of a sudden he became a racist. When Senator Trent Lott praised Senator Thurmond for some of his accomplishments late in life, Senator Lott was condemned by Democrats for supporting racism. The point to note is that the defining behavior for racism is not your attitude toward people with a different skin tone. It's your political party affiliation!

Another example occurred here in Colorado in 2005, when former U.S. Senator Hank Brown was being considered as a candidate for interim President of the University of Colorado. President Betsy Hoffman had announced her resignation, and candidates were being considered for the position she had just vacated. Senator Brown is a Republican, and state Senator Peter Groff, a Democrat, was quoted as being disturbed about Senator Brown's concern for people with dark skin color: "I wanted to make sure there was a commitment to diversity...I wasn't sure the senator had a commitment at a level that was high enough for my issues or my concerns," said Groff.

The University of Colorado, under President Hoffman, had less than two percent black students in its undergraduate student body. To my knowledge, she was never criticized for a lack of emphasis on diversity. When Senator Brown's name was tendered, however, the concern voiced by Senator Groff was that of racism.

Fortunately for Hank Brown, he had a very public record of affirmative action initiatives from his tenure as President of the University of Northern Colorado. He wrote Senator Groff a letter that outlined these programs, and the accusations of racism died down.

The problem is that most of us aren't like Hank Brown, and don't have a record of public achievements in affirmative action. We end up being like Laura Bush, and simply respond that the accusations leave us "disgusted".

Let's move on to the second part of the "Republicans are bad people" theme: Republicans are homophobic. You will find that the same point can be made in regards to being homophobic: There are simply no homophobic Democrats. Homophobia is a purely Republican phenomenon.

Homophobia normally relates to those individuals who have a prejudice against homosexual people. It speaks of a person having a fear of the diversity within the human race. However, in a manner similar to the use of the word "disenfranchise", the term takes on a vastly expanded meaning in the Democrat Party. Here the term becomes the well spring for the darkest characteristics of Republicans. Homophobic Republicans have deep personality flaws. They embrace torture! They join the military and become the enemy of humanity! They are capable of the most despicable acts!

I know it sounds far-fetched, but this is where you will see the Hitler/Nazi/Fascist references. If you are a Republican and choose to run for public office, gird your loins! At some point the Democrat Party will accuse you of having some sort of Nazi tendency. It has simply become an expected part of our political discourse.

Not always are the accusations or the characterizations so extreme. There are subtle manifestations. I've noticed, for example, that if a Republican is being introduced to a gay couple, the person doing the introductions will often quietly make sure that the person of the Republican persuasion is made aware that the people he or she is going to meet are gay. While it appears to be a kind and gentle thing to do, it carries the implication that the Republican in question would tend to behave inappropriately if the sexual orientation issue were not explicitly covered. It is a "caring" put-down, but it is a put-down none the less.

You will also find that the word "homophobic" is essentially a pejorative, used much in the vein of the word "Conservative". It allows us to think disparagingly of Republicans. If you are a Republican, you will implicitly be considered homophobic and racist. It is a part of our American culture.

So now we're getting close to the end. The third and final part of the "Republicans are bad people" theme deals with bigotry. If you are a Democrat, you are not bigoted. It is essentially a Republican trait, and it brings in the religious component of the debate.

The dictionary definition of the word "bigot" relates to intolerance for the beliefs of others, including political and ethnic beliefs. However, the Democrat Party uses this term as a code word for the manner in which members of "The Religious Right" hold to their Christian values and beliefs. The idea is that if you are evangelical in your approach to your faith, you clearly have to be intolerant of others. Again, the word is used as a pejorative, and it does not make sense to try to point out all the ways you are tolerant when the Democrat Party refers to you as a bigot. We'll go into greater detail on this issue later on. (The interrelationship between politics and religion is worth a chapter of its own.)

Racism, homophobia, and bigotry: these are the components of the "Republicans are bad people" theme. I realize there are many other ways to describe Republicans as "bad". President Bush is called a liar, a moron, and a miserable failure. Republicans are generally depicted as insensitive, self-absorbed and uncaring. Do you need an "in your face" example? Take a look at political cartoons to see if they reflect the anti-Republican culture. Don't take for granted that a cartoon is simply innocent non-partisan fun. They actively support the anti-Republican themes, and they tend to reinforce that most basic of themes: Republicans are just plainly bad people.

I have just one final point to emphasize on this first theme. It often appears in its softer form: REPUBLICANS ARE MEAN-SPIRITED. I used this phrase at the start of this section, and I'll bet you read right over it. Don't be misled by the terminology. It is not an attempt to understand the spiritual being of Republicans. You will not find many instances of people from the Democratic Party being characterized as mean-spirited. The term is applied almost exclusively to Republicans, and it is meant to quietly convey the "Republicans are bad people" theme.

REPUBLICANS ARE DESTROYING THE ENVIRONMENT

The second theme I'll talk about is the one that gets me the most agitated. I'll not spend too much time on it, but this is the one that really gets to me. It makes me mad.

I was born in Oregon, in the town of Roseburg. I can remember our radio station claiming that "Roseburg is the timber capital of the nation!" I had an uncle that worked in the forests, running a motorized device called a "donkey". It was used to drag logs up the side of a mountain to a location where the logs were subsequently loaded onto trucks. It was over fifty years ago, and it was a time that provided strong before-and-after pictures of a forest being literally stripped of timber in accommodating the demand for lumber.

Americans have come a long way in the last fifty years. We now think of our forests as renewable resources that need care, not something that we can destroy and abandon. I like to believe that the idea of "leaving the land we occupy in better shape than we found it" is a common sentiment shared by most Americans. While I think a poll surveying environmental attitudes would overwhelmingly show that sense of "husbandry", I would accept a response rate of 70% or greater as being enough affirmation. We simply value our planet and feel the need to protect it.

So this is a "non-issue", right? Not so fast. Perhaps the strongest and most frequent theme of the Democrat party is that Republicans are destroying the environment. It starts early. In Colorado we had a recent instance of an elementary school teacher having her students write their Republican congressman and implore him to stop polluting the environment. In our political contests, the Democratic candidates will emphasize they are "for the environment"; leaving the lingering implication that Republican opponents are against the environment. In the 2004 race for U. S. Senator in Colorado, Pete Coors, the Republican candidate, had an advertisement run against him that featured dead fish. A Coors employee accidentally discharged fermenting beer into Clear Creek, suffocating fish in the stream below the accident site. While this would seem to be an industrial accident to some observers, it became a pitch by the Democrat party to illustrate how Pete Coors hurts the Colorado environment. It may not have been a fair characterization, but it worked.

And why does it work? It is because the theme of Republicans destroying the environment is accepted in our culture. It is a "given".

The theme has gotten new legs with the global warming

issue. Here, the abstraction of the concept lends itself particularly well to the anti-Republican culture. Just as Republicans "don't care" about black people, they don't care about the environment. It's the abstract nature of the issue that allows it to become a political weapon, and it is being used to demonstrate how insensitive and out-of-touch Republicans are. As I said, I get agitated over this issue. It seems totally unfair to cast millions of people as being "against the environment", but in our anti-Republican culture, it works.

REPUBLICANS ARE HARMING OUR CHILDREN

This theme is loaded with emotion. It incorporates a broader view of children, from birth all the way to the twenty-something age group. Here you will find examples of young children having to bear the stigma of standardized testing. A little further along will be children reaching puberty and having to deal with the trauma of abortion politics. Even later in the age group comes the wrenching emotional grappling with very adult issues such as the military draft.

The perception that runs through the "harming our children" theme is that the problems are catastrophic. Having to engage in standardized testing ensures problems with self esteem and self actualization. It's not simply that you as a child have to endure the testing, it's that you are having to conform to a standard. This may cause you to feel inadequate (in the case where you don't do well on the test) or to be destroyed in your life's quest (in the case where the tests cause a detour in your prospective area of study). The idea that the tests help measure the effectiveness of teaching seems to get lost in the political milieu.

The issue of children and abortion politics is, if not a catastrophe, certainly extremely troubling. Here we compound the tragedy of a pregnant youngster with the political issues of parental notification, involvement by institutions, and the rights of people who are not yet adults. You would think that an unexpected pregnancy in a young female would be a time for nurturing and support. Unfortunately, it is too ripe a target for political action. The children get caught in the crossfire, with Republicans being cast as the villains.

The final childhood catastrophe exploited by the Democrat Party is the extension of "children status" to those people joining the military. Even after the age of 18, if you voluntarily join the military you are assumed to be exercising flawed, child-like judgment. The idea is that no adult in their right mind would choose to enter the military voluntarily.

This one actually makes sense on a gut level. The desire for peace is a universal human need. The aberration is the person who wishes to engage in war and killing. What doesn't feel right is to say that those who wish to participate in the military are in favor of warfare. There is a difference between working to prevent or minimize the extent of warfare and working to encourage and engage in warfare. I don't think anti-war advocates understand that difference.

Regardless, it is all an issue of politics, and depicting someone as being a person who wants to draft people, engage in warfare, and generally behave in an anti-social manner is a little over the top even in politics. It is more elegant to simply depict the person as being one who wants to harm our children.

REPUBLICANS ARE STEALING FROM OUR SENIORS

This is a theme that comes and goes. In general, the wealth of our country is controlled by older people, so it would make sense to assume that if anyone is stealing from someone, they would steal from those with the money. However, the approach used by the Democrat Party is to cast Republicans as the ones stealing from those least able to protect themselves: the elderly.

What is being stolen? Principally it is Social Security benefits and prescription drug benefits. How does the theft occur? By changing systems that have been in place for a long time. Entitlement programs become programs that people depend upon, and to take away that upon which you depend is stealing of the worst sort. Thieving Republicans are to blame.

Watch for examples made of people who have to adjust their lifestyles because of sickness or infirmity. Republicans may not be the cause of the sickness or infirmity, but the strong impression will be left that Republicans make the plight worse, and in fact seem to rejoice in the problems they cause. You will see the technique of using anecdotal evidence to represent widespread problems. A person will be caught in the "donut hole" of prescription drug benefits. (Never mind that the individual is paying less for prescription drugs than he or she did before. Just keep in mind that the person is having to suffer because of the inept Republican antics.) Another individual will explain how the uncertainty of Social Security benefits causes them great personal stress. (Never mind that the individual is adequately covered. Simply take note of the pain and anguish the Republicans are causing.)

Older people are not the most disadvantaged and impoverished group in the United States, but that will not be the impression provided by the Democrat Party.

REPUBLICANS ARE SHREDDING THE CONSTITUTION

This is a theme that hinges on perceptions. From a Republican Party standpoint, the Constitution of the United States is a revered document. I don't mean that in a cynical sense. Republicans do tend to view the Constitution as something very special. (They actually think the Founding Fathers really knew what they were doing.) The Constitution ends up being both flexible and rigid. It elegantly lays out principles of governance without having to define them in minute detail. It creates a sense of ownership for all Americans, simply by being something that is valuable and needs to be protected. For a document that is short in length, it is really quite an amazing piece of work.

To the Democrat Party, the Constitution is a prop. Going back to our earlier analogy, the Constitution is simply a theatrical item used to make melodramatic points on the stage of American politics. It can be a good thing or a bad thing. Let's look at a few examples.

Suppose that you are interested in the Presidency of the United States being an elected office that is determined by a nationwide vote of individuals rather than a vote of the states making up the country. You think that the Presidency should be determined by the overall popular vote, rather than the sum of the electoral votes of the 50 states.

There are two ways to approach the problem: work with the Constitution and amend it, or take the easier route of working around the Constitution. If you felt that the Constitution had special significance, you would be inclined to work the problem by amending the Constitution. If you felt the Constitution were more of a prop, you might avoid amending the Constitution and simply work to have each state cast its electoral votes for the winner of the popular vote throughout the country. That would change the intent of the Constitution, without having to change the Constitution in the manner it sets forth. Simply by getting each state (particularly the less populace ones) to cast their electoral votes in a certain fashion, you get the job done.

And here is where the difference in perception comes in. The Democrat Party would argue that the Constitution has an inherent role in promoting democracy, and a country-wide vote is pure democracy. The Republican Party would say that the Constitution speaks for itself. While the Constitution recognizes the ideals of democracy, it sets up a representative government with powers vested in states. Republicans might say, "Simply look at the language of the Constitution, and do what it says."

In the eyes of the Democrat Party, the Constitution is sometimes bad for the country and sometimes good. It depends on whether the Constitution gets interpreted in favor of Republicans or Democrats.

The outcome of the 2000 Presidential Election is perhaps the best case in point. It captured many of the themes of the Democratic Party. We saw the "Republicans are stealing from seniors" theme, with older voters claiming their votes were accidentally placed for the Republican candidate when they meant to vote for the Democrat. We had the "Republicans are racists" theme with stories of people with dark skin color having difficulty getting to polling booths. We had the "Republicans are bigots" theme, with Republicans unable to understand how "making every vote count" translated into the divining of the intentions of voters submitting blank ballots, partially punched ballots, and dual-punched ballots. It seemed that any spoiled ballot was really a sign of a voter doing his or her best to vote for a Democratic candidate.

But the big one was the "Republicans are shredding the Constitution" theme. This came about when the Republican Party thought it was unfair to have recounts done in selected Florida counties without applying uniform rules across those counties. The idea being that giving unequal treatment to voters within a state violated the Equal Protection Clause of the 14th Amendment to the Constitution. There was no "shredding of the Constitution" when the Florida Supreme Court said that the unequal treatment was okay. The problem came when the decision was appealed, and the Supreme Court of the United States ruled that the unequal treatment was NOT okay.

Suddenly, Republicans were guilty of Constitutional shenanigans. They had trampled on the Constitution by allowing the Supreme Court of the United States to determine the outcome of an election. Republicans not only weren't letting every vote count, they were shredding the Constitution!

It's interesting to me that a similar legal challenge occurred in Colorado's 2004 election for the Congressional Representative of District 7. There was a flaw in the counting of provisional ballots. The Congressional District spanned parts of three counties, and the provisional ballots used by the counties were not counted in the same fashion. The Democratic Party sued, in the same fashion that the Republican Party sued in the 2000 presidential election. This time the Republicans lost, but the good news is that in both cases, our highest courts upheld the validity of the Equal Protection Clause.

So what does all of this mean? It means that a person needs to do some research whenever you hear that "Republicans are shredding the Constitution". It is a claim that is often made when a court decision goes against the Democratic Party, and is an accusation made whenever the Democratic Party is using the Constitution as a prop. Watch for it when the Democratic Party wishes to attach Constitutional Rights to non-citizens. You will find that it makes little difference what specific language exists in the Constitution. The Democratic Party will cite the Constitution in cases of rights for illegal immigrants and enemy combatants. It doesn't matter that the Constitution is essentially a document that spells out what our federal government can and cannot do. The Democratic Party will use the Constitution to promote certain behaviors and attitudes. Whenever the Republican Party takes exception to these views, out comes the accusation of "shredding the Constitution". It makes the melodrama interesting.

REPUBLICANS ARE TURNING THE ECONOMY INTO A CATASTROPHE

You would think that the behavior of the United States economy would be essentially non-political: "It is what it is." Organizations like the U. S. Commerce Department or the Bureau of Labor Statistics simply collect economic data and report it. Data may be reported as "preliminary" and be subsequently revised, but the idea is to make it accurate and consistent so that it can be compared to historical data and conclusions can be drawn. It is not meant to be a political football.

That being said, the problem with economic data is that (thanks to people like Milton Friedman and John Maynard Keynes) we now know that monetary policy and fiscal policy have far-reaching effects on our individual lives. Monetary policy (using interest rates and credit availability to influence the quantity of money available to us) and fiscal policy (using taxation and government spending to influence our consumption) can cause our economy to boom or bust. Understanding their effects can help us know when to refinance a home or bail out of the stock market. It's important stuff!

Where does the political dimension come in? It happens with the time delays associated with economic policies. Things don't happen overnight. If you lower taxes to stimulate the economy, you don't see the effects for a couple of years. If you increase government spending to stimulate the economy, you create deficits that carry over to the next generation and "saddle our children with debt". In a nutshell, doing what needs to be done for the health of the economy may not be what needs to be done to ensure political survival.

Even so, there are still things we know are true and can count on. For example, when the economy is recovering from a recession, a leading indicator is a turn in the stock market. Employment numbers, however, won't improve for several more months. Employment will NEVER be a leading indicator. It just makes sense that employment follows a turnaround in economic expectations. You wouldn't hire new employees unless you expected business to improve, and a lot of business people have learned to wait until they are sure business is improving before they start hiring.

Because the economy is always changing, there is always news to convey to a waiting public. Why not use it to advance a political agenda? Here's where the "Republicans are turning the economy into a catastrophe" theme comes in. It turns economic reporting into political sport. I'll provide an example to help illustrate the point.

Below are two news releases from two separate news organizations. The first is from an Associated Press story posted on the Internet by Yahoo! News:

CONSUMER CONFIDENCE FALLS ON JOB WORRIES
By Anne D'Innocenzio, AP Business Writer
7/26/05
 NEW YORK – Renewed worries about the economy and jobs sent consumer confidence downward in July, breaking a three-month winning streak.
 The Conference Board said Tuesday its Consumer Confidence Index fell to 103.2 from a revised 106.2 in June. The July figure was worse than the 106.2 analysts expected.
 In May, the index rose to 103.1 from April's 97.5.
 Lynn Franco, director of the private research group's Consumer Research Center, said the dip was "no cause for

concern."

"The overall state of the economy remains healthy and consumers' outlook suggests no storm clouds on the short-term horizon," Franco said in a statement. "Even the steady upward tick of fuel prices at the pump has done relatively little to dampen consumers' spirits. Yet, while there is little to suggest a downturn in activity, there is also little to suggest a pickup."

One component of the consumer confidence report, which looks at consumers' views of the current economic situation, fell to 118.5 from 120.8. Another component, the Expectations Index, which measures consumers' outlook over the next six months, declined to 93.0 percent from 96.4 in June.

The Conference Board's gauges are derived from responses received through July 19 to a survey mailed to 5,000 households in a consumer research panel. The figures released Tuesday include responses from at least 2,500 households.

The outlook for the labor market was mixed. The number of consumers expecting more jobs to become available in the coming months edged up to 15.8 percent from 15.4 percent, while those expecting fewer jobs moved up to 16.8 percent from 16.4 percent in June. The proportion of consumers anticipating their incomes will increase in the months ahead declined to 18.6 percent from 19.9 percent.

Consumers' overall assessment of ongoing conditions was somewhat mixed in July. The number of those claiming business conditions are "bad" increased to 16.9 percent from 15.3 percent. However, those saying conditions are "good" improved to 28.7 percent from 26.7 percent.

The employment picture was also mixed. Consumers saying jobs are "hard to get" rose to 23.8 percent from 22.5 percent, but those claiming jobs are "plentiful" remained at 22.5 percent.

Consumers' outlook for the next six months was marginally less favorable than in June. Those expecting business conditions to improve fell to 17.6 percent from 19.5 percent. Consumers anticipating that business conditions will worsen edged up to 9.6 percent from 9.0 percent.

The second story appeared in the *Rocky Mountain News* Business Section (page 9B) on July 27, 2005:

CONSUMER CONFIDENCE DIP 'NO CAUSE FOR CONCERN'

Americans' anxiety about the economy and their jobs resurfaced in July, sending a widely followed measure of consumer confidence downward and ending a three-month winning streak.

The Conference Board said Tuesday its consumer confidence index fell to 103.2 from a revised 106.2 in June.

The July figure was worse than the 106.2 analysts expected. In May, the index rose to 103.1 from April's 97.5.

Lynn Franco, director of the private research group's Consumer Research Center, said the dip was "no cause for concern."

"The overall state of the economy remains healthy and consumers' outlook suggests no storm clouds on the short-term horizon," Franco said in a statement.

"Even the steady upward tick of fuel prices at the pump has done relatively little to dampen consumers' spirits.

"Yet, while there is little to suggest a downturn in activity, there is also little to suggest a pickup," he said.

Consumers' sentiment contrasted with an upbeat assessment of the economy last week from Federal Reserve Chairman Alan Greenspan.

Greenspan said he expected the economy to keep growing even as a flurry of job cuts from major corporations were announced.

In both stories, if you ignore the headline and the first sentence, the next six sentences are exactly the same. Evidently the Conference Board released its monthly survey results, and the Rocky Mountain News and Yahoo! News posted those results in the text of their stories.

What's interesting about each story is not the text within the story, but the headline and the lead-in to the story. It struck me that there was not much news in the report, but it provided an opportunity to hit the public with a standard anti-Republican theme. Because we keep hearing that Republicans are turning the economy into a catastrophe, we expect to hear that job prospects are a problem.

Ms. D'Innocenzio, reporting for the AP, notes in the text of her piece that "The outlook for the labor market was mixed." She also notes that "The employment picture was also mixed." However, the headline doesn't refer to anything about mixed results. It states that "Consumer Confidence Falls on Job Worries". The Democrat Party knows that "Job Worries" is an emotionally-charged term. It implies Republican failures and gets placed in headlines as often as possible. In the case of Yahoo! News, the headline writer took advantage of the opportunity. The Rocky Mountain News let it pass.

You'll have to take my word for it, but these two economic news stories are actually fairly minor examples of "spin" in a news story. You will be able to find much more interesting examples just in reading a daily newspaper or surfing the Internet. In fact, I've wondered if any post-secondary school ever tries playing the game "Guess the Headline" to see if students can fathom the inner workings of headline writers. The way the game is played is to present students with examples of text from various news stories of the day, but remove the headline and lead-in to the story. Based upon the content of the story, the students would then list their best guess for the headline to the story.

What would be the outcome of the exercise? My guess is that you'd find most of the student headline suggestions would relate to the content of the story in some specific way, perhaps using a catchy turn of phrase. When you then see the headline that is actually used on the story, it brings the anti-Republican perspective of the headline writer into sharp focus.

Once the students get the hang of the game, a more sophisticated exercise is to get them to try to write a headline that mirrors the style exhibited by the headline writer for the news service they are examining. As they learn how to match the tone and style, they get a solid understanding of the technique used to set anti-Republican themes to news stories.

For extra credit, students might be invited to analyze the political party affiliations glossed over in the news stories. Here you will have to get away from the Business section of the newspaper and look more at the World News section or the front page itself. Whenever you see phrases like, "informed sources say..." or "a bi-partisan group acknowledged..." see how the tone of the story changes if the political party affiliation of the group is disclosed.

Would the meaning change if instead of "informed sources say..." the text actually read, "informed sources, all of whom are Democrats, say..."? Or what if the phrase "a bi-partisan group..." actually read, "a bi-partisan group of one Republican and 23 Democrats..."?

I think critical readers of news stories implicitly do this. They look for a "false consensus" to be presented, where the story implies that everyone believes a certain way, or feels a certain way. They also look for selective quotes, where it might be noted that two points of view are presented, but the "money quote" comes from just one side of the debate. It takes a little extra effort, but once you start doing it, there is no going back. You get hooked.

You start to show tendencies of becoming a "political junkie".

5

ULTRA AFFIRMATIVE ACTION

Do you have any "political junkie" tendencies? The next few chapters are going to test you.

I don't know about you, but I need a break from all this anti-Republican stuff. Maybe we can lighten up a bit by looking at the ways the Democrat Party can help Republicans move into the "Good People" category. This takes us into the "Just for Fun" chapters, and we'll get started with an improbable anecdote about the politics of drafting young people into the military.

Former Senator Fritz Hollings (D-SC) and Representative Charlie Rangel (D-NY) submitted bills in the House and the Senate in 2003 to reinstate the military draft. The idea was to draft young men and women between the ages of 18 and 26 for military service to help us meet our worldwide military commitments. The military draft had been abolished in 1973, but Senator Hollings and Representative Rangel felt it was important to bring it back, this time with a provision to draft women.

Republicans pretty much dismissed the bills with a collective "Huh?" They knew that the United States military is made up of an all-volunteer force. The idea of a draft might be a great way to get more people working as government employees (with draft boards sprouting up all across the country) but to put in a massive government program to add a few thousand recruits to the armed forces? It didn't make sense.

What did make sense was the politics of the maneuver. It allowed Democrats to talk about efforts to bring back the draft. On college campuses, young voters were warned of a coming "January Surprise" where draft boards would be calling them if they voted for a Republican president. Young female voters were told that there was a very real possibility the draft would affect them. Republicans were characterized as "Chicken Hawks" because they verbally supported the efforts in Iraq, but hadn't personally sent their sons or daughters off to war. The intent of the draft would be to make sure the Chicken Hawks had a personal stake in the war, and perhaps would be less inclined to support warfighting if their own kids were in danger of being drafted.

The House bill was brought to a vote in October of 2004, just before the election, and was defeated on a roll call vote of 402 to 2. Even Charlie Rangel didn't vote for it. His own bill! Think about that for a moment. A Congressman goes to the trouble to author a bill only to vote against it! One could legitimately ask the question "Is this political posturing?"

THE WHITE MALE DRAFT

Let's pursue this a bit further. We'll assume that the idea of drafting young people has merit. Let's also assume that the Democratic Party is sincerely interested in bringing about societal change: They feel there is an inherent need to change the balance between races in America! They feel America needs Social Engineering!

Affirmative Action has been the primary tool to change racial balance, but it never seems to go far enough for the Democratic Party. A truly effective way to solve this problem is needed. America must have an Ultra-Affirmative Action Program! We need a White Male Draft!

Here's the way the program would be configured: All white males between the ages of 16 and 26 would be drafted.

You're wondering, "Is that all there is to it?" Well, yes, it's a pretty simple program. The program would be run by the Democrat Party, and would require every white male in

America to register by his 16th birthday. From that point until he reaches his 26th birthday, his education and employment would be governed by the Democrat Party. Take note that I am using the term "Democrat Party" here. This is the group that embodies the soul of the Democratic Party ideology. This is where Democratic ideology has its most prominent proponents.

Anyway, here's another interesting detail: Each draftee would create a "Dream Sheet" that would include his top three choices for education and employment. To the extent possible, the Democrat Party would give the individual one of his three top choices, but that might not always be possible. Depending on the needs of the Democrat Party, the individual could be placed anywhere within the American educational or workforce structure to enhance societal and economic goals.

Think about it! If the country does not have enough women in college, the white male draftees would be restricted from enrolling in college. The percentage of women in college would immediately go up, and the percentage could be fine-tuned to meet the expectations of the Democrat Party. What about people with dark skin color? If the country does not have enough doctors or lawyers with dark skin color, draftees would be kept out of medical school or law school. The percentages of minorities in those professions could be controlled with a great degree of precision, to get just the right societal mix!

What about the military? The Democrat Party feels that the military has too high a percentage of people with dark skin color? No problem! The military could be loaded up with white males.

Keep in mind that the restrictions on education and employment only apply to males with white skin tones, so there might be some problems in getting the correct mix of ethnic and racial balance, since everyone except white males would be able to choose his or her direction in life without restriction. Also, the draft would expire when the draftee reaches the age of 26, so there would also be the problem of older Caucasian males competing for professional schooling and related careers. But keep in mind the goal here. We can work to engineer a perfect society! Just because the results may not be perfect is not a valid reason for abandoning the ideal.

Could a White Male Draft exist in our country? Probably not. But it is an interesting mental exercise to think of, in terms of what changes we would make to our institutions if we could control them with precision. If we could create a society of just the right racial and ethnic mix, what would it look like? It's almost like the Global Warming debate. If we could control our climate, what would the right mix of moisture and sunlight look like?

And maybe the larger question is, "Would controlling our society and environment with precision create happiness?" Would we eliminate racism? Would we eliminate strife?

It comes down to basic philosophies about human existence in our world: Is our day-to-day living better-served by a controlling authority or better served by freedom of choice? You can probably tell my bias here, but you've got to admit the idea has some appeal. What if we needed more players with dark skin color in the National Basketball Association? The White Male Draft would take care of it. Maybe our employment numbers are a bit too low? Take draftees out of colleges and put them into Public Works projects. Voila! Jobs are created regardless of the state of the economy!

And note the most important part: The Democrat Party is totally in charge of the White Male Draft. There is no need for consensus. Whatever the Democrat Party thinks is the right mix is what gets put in place! We will actually see the fruits of social engineering as envisioned by the Democrat Party. Their vision for equality in America would be implemented without constraint. The necessity for properly engineering our society would trump all other requirements.

How to measure the results? We simply watch what changes occur once draftees reach age 26 and are no longer governed by the principles of the Democrat Party. Do they embrace the behavior previously mandated for them, or do they turn away from it? Does racial harmony result or do we end up with deepening resentment? Do they perceive the need to get a proper mix of skin tones as a valid societal goal? Does the vision of the Democrat Party outweigh freedom of choice in America?

Americans will let us know.

6

FOR RICHER, FOR POORER

Let's get back to the themes we were discussing. Aside from the Bad Republican theme, there were themes related to the environment, children, seniors, the Constitution, and our economy. One of the more common Democratic Party criticisms related to the economy is that Republicans favor the rich to the detriment of the poor. It's what you might term "Robin Hood Politics". Republicans are cast as the ones who are taking away school lunches, removing healthcare resources from kids, and making our older citizens choose between heating their homes, having food on the table, or taking prescription medicines. If you have a Republican political affiliation, you no longer care for the disadvantaged of our society. Republicans apparently have an inherent desire to hurt the less fortunate. We have no sense of charity or compassion!

But there is hope. The Democrat Party can be vested with powers that will change all of that.

THE EXCESS WEALTH AND INCOME TAX

The problem with older people in America is that they are not all the same. While there are people aged 60 and over who are in difficult times, there are also people in this age group who are doing quite well. In fact, some of them are doing VERY WELL. These are the people that the Democratic Party refers to as "The Rich".

I realize that there are younger people who have done

well for themselves, and many of them happen to be in show business or are playing professional sports. However, it somehow seems inappropriate to turn on someone who is very popular and making lots of money. You might think that they have achieved too much too soon, but life can be filled with unexpected twists and turns, and a younger person might end up penniless by the time he or she reaches the age of sixty. If that were the case, it would be unseemly to deprive them of their joy early on, only to find out life deals them even greater difficulties in the later years. The right thing to do is to wait until they have passed the age of sixty. At that point, they become subject to the Excess Wealth and Income Tax.

This is another program that would be strictly and totally run by the Democrat Party. Again, there is no need to achieve consensus. What the Democrat Party thinks is the right thing to do is what gets done. Here is how it would work:

First, there are no hard and fast definitions. The level at which one becomes "rich" does not have to be set in advance. It certainly entails levels of income and levels of assets, but the Democrat Party does not need to explicitly define these levels. Being rich or being poor is simply something that one "knows when he or she sees it".

So how would it play out? Let's say that you are an American who has reached the age of sixty. At that point, your assets and income are subject to Democrat Party review. Your tax forms would change to where you don't just report income, but you also report assets. If during the prior years you had worked to accumulate too much wealth, or you are currently earning too much income, the excess would be subject to the Excess Wealth and Income Tax. It would be levied by the Democrat Party, and would be due and payable when the Democrat Party says it is due.

What would be done with the money? The Democrat Party apportions it back to individuals based upon their needs. Thus, the Excess Wealth and Income Tax becomes the way for the Democrat Party to do away with the misfortunes of our children and Seniors. It is a "Robin Hood effect", without a

Sheriff of Nottingham. The Democrat Party takes care of the redistribution of wealth, with the necessary money coming from those who can afford to give it up.

I think the only requirement to make this concept a reality is a reporting requirement. The Democrat Party would have to disclose where the money comes from and where it goes. If there is a need to avoid a problem with "taxation without representation", the Democrat Party could provide a list of the potential "Rich Taxpayers" to Congress, and they could vote on who is taxed.

It seems to be a pretty good idea, and it certainly has some appealing features. Let's look just at the "Excess Income" part of the tax. You don't necessarily have to restrict this to people who are sixty years of age and older. It could apply to anyone making too much money.

The Democrat Party would work the income problems in our country from two sides: There would be thresholds at both ends of the spectrum. For example, you could ensure that anyone submitting a tax form receives a minimum amount of income. If I submit a form saying I made $4,000.00 in a given year, and the Democrat Party threshold for minimum income is $10,000.00, then I would get a "refund" of $6,000.00 after submitting my tax form. Thus it would set a floor on the minimum amount earned by an American tax filer. There would be no tax filer who would make less than $10,000.00 per year. We could eliminate poverty!

How would we tax the rich? Just as there is a floor on the minimum amount of money an American tax filer would need, there would be a ceiling on the maximum amount of money an American tax filer could make. If you happened to make $11 million in a given year, and the maximum set by the Democrat Party is $10 million, then the extra $1 million would be the amount of your Excess Income Tax. Income in America would be bracketed, so that people would never earn more than a certain amount, and would never earn less than a certain amount. The gap could be narrowed until there is no more poverty and there is no more "obscene profit". The

Democrat Party could gradually move us toward a perfect society, and they could start with "baby steps": Take only from the very rich, and give only to the very poor. Start small, but then continue onward, closing the income gap by reducing the extremes at either end.

What about the Excess Wealth side of the plan? Here I do think you've got to stand firm on the age threshold. We've got a model for the Excess Wealth Tax in the form of our Estate Tax, which kicks in upon the death of the taxpayer. But I've got to think it would be discouraging (to say the least) if you had to fill out, and be subject to, a wealth tax form every year of your taxpaying life. It would make sense to give the individual some time to achieve a state of wealth before taxing that wealth. Maybe the threshold date gets changed over time, but start at the age of sixty for the taxpayer.

What about the issue of frequency? How often to you assess the Excess Wealth Tax? It's pretty hard to make multiple fortunes in a lifetime, and it would be discouraging if each time you finally get ahead, the Democrat Party takes your wealth away. For this reason, the Excess Wealth Tax should only be assessed once in a lifetime. This has the advantage of delivering a severe wound to the Golden Goose, but not necessarily killing it.

How much tax should apply to a wealthy individual? Let's take as an example the wife of Senator John Kerry, Teresa Heinz. If she had the Excess Wealth Tax applied to her, what would be the appropriate assessment? Should it be a percentage of her wealth, or should her wealth be reduced to a certain threshold? Let's say the goal is to make everyone in the United States have no more than $1 million in wealth. If Teresa starts with $500 million in assets, and that gets reduced to $1 million, that's a $499 million hit and a 99.8% tax rate. That gets her to the level of everyone else, but is it fair to take away 99.8% of her wealth? If instead her wealth is reduced to $250 million, that's still a $250 million hit and a 50% tax rate, but she keeps $250 million. Is that too much? She's still rich! To most of us, these amounts are so large that they become abstract. To Teresa, though, this is real money! The way in which the Excess Wealth Tax is levied becomes a big deal!

The whole issue seems to be wrapped up in the concept of fairness. For the individual, probably the fair thing to do is to reduce each rich person's wealth by the same percentage. For society, it might make sense to reduce everyone in the "rich" category to a certain level of wealth. The Democrat Party could proclaim that it has reduced the wealth of the rich so that, "There are no American billionaires!" Or maybe go all the way to where there are no American millionaires. It could be possible to change income and wealth in America to where there are no rich people and there is no poverty. It's just a matter of getting the proper redistribution of wealth and income, and settling on definitions of "the rich" and "the poor". The Democrat Party becomes the champion of "Robin Hood Politics".

Like the White Male Draft, a system of income redistribution through an Excess Wealth and Income Tax is probably not going to happen in America. It's not because the idea of Robin Hood Politics is unpopular, but rather because it's a difficult system to implement. The fairness issue is the most problematic. Fairness between individuals and fairness within a society are often in conflict. Think about trying to apply it just within your own extended family. If you've got a deadbeat relative who is never going to get ahead, and a star performer who is the family favorite, how do you take money from one and give to the other with a sense of fairness? What if the family favorite became wealthy through lottery winnings? What if the winner was poor up until the winning ticket was drawn? What if the winner was already well-off prior to the winning ticket being drawn? Who in the family gets more and who gets less? Who gets to be the decision maker?

What if the family favorite earned the money by foregoing luxuries and making sacrifices all of his or her life? Now the favored one reaches age sixty and it is time to make the distribution. Because the excess wealth was obtained through sacrifice, does that impact the decision to take it away? What if the wealthy person sees the tax coming and decides to move to Canada to avoid the tax?

I think the fairness issue is what kills the concept. For whatever reason, we seem to be ok with the idea of having a wealth tax that gets applied upon the death of a person, but to have such a tax applied during life just seems to have a lot of problems. The Democrat Party will continue to accuse Republicans of favoring the rich and abandoning the poor, but it will keep the idea of wealth redistribution as an abstract concept. To actually put an Excess Wealth and Income Tax into practice would just cause too much brain damage for everyone.

7

SAVE THE CHILDREN

Here is a poll question:

"Do you support or reject the idea of owning and controlling a portion of your Social Security contributions?"

Let's say 100 people are given that question, and 50 say they support the idea and 50 say they reject it. Now, we'll make a small change to the polling question. Here's the new language:

"Do you support or reject the Republican idea of owning and controlling a portion of your Social Security contributions?"

We "politicized" the second question. How do you think it will affect the results? My expectation is that the number of respondents saying they support the idea will decrease. That's our anti-Republican culture at work. If you wish to shade an outcome one way or another, play on the anti-Republican sentiment in our culture. Simply adding a Republican connotation, even without using specific references, will color the results.

Our society seems to have very little interest in determining the nature and extent of the anti-Republican sentiment in our culture. But wouldn't it be interesting to find out which American age-group is most charged with the anti-Republican emotions? I would imagine it is in the 20 to 40-year age group, just based on personal observation. But when exactly does it begin? We certainly aren't born being anti-Republican. The behavior is learned.

By the time you are in your twenties, you are clearly aware

of political influences. More than likely, at the age of 18, you were confronted with the issue of declaring a political party, whether Republican, Democrat or something else. But what is your earliest exposure to political preferences?

I know that my grandmother was a Republican, but I am just assuming my grandfather was a Republican. He died before I was in grade school, and I wasn't aware of how politics fit into his life. I'm pretty sure I didn't care about politics one way or another when I was in grade school.

What if that changed? What if there were a Democrat Children's Movement in place?

THE DEMOCRAT CHILDREN'S MOVEMENT

On an informal basis, this program already exists. In Colorado, Representative Tom Tancredo received letters and drawings from the students of one of his constituents who was a grade school teacher. The students were requesting that he stop poisoning the water, ruining our forests, and killing animals. It was a bit troubling, and seemed to indicate that youngsters in at least one classroom in Colorado were being taught that Republicans are destroying the environment. It seems as if our children are being indoctrinated at a fairly early age.

At the High School level, a Geography instructor in Colorado lectured on the pervasiveness of American violence in the world. His point was that the United States is probably the most violent nation on Earth.

This on its face may not seem like indoctrination, but a bit of background knowledge gives a different perspective. Note that the idea presented is that a particular country is portrayed as being prone to violence, and that the prime candidate is the United States of America. The perspective to note is that other countries have engaged in violent acts in their domestic and foreign affairs, but that the individual country is typically not blamed. Rather, it is the country's ruling body that gets singled out.

Take as an example the country of Cambodia. You rarely hear of Cambodia being characterized as a violent country.

Instead, you hear of the two million people killed by the Khmer Rouge during four years of the Pol Pot regime. The same perspective applies to countries such as Russia and Germany where the countries themselves are not depicted as being violent, but the violence is attributed to the regimes of Stalin, Hitler and so on.

Here are some figures relating to the human cost of United States military actions, with military deaths rounded down to the nearest 10,000:

--The Civil War (550,000 military deaths) began when a Democrat (Jefferson Davis) took the southern states and seceded from the Union.

--World War I (110,000 military deaths) began when Woodrow Wilson (a Democrat) was president.

--World War II (400,000 military deaths) began when Franklin Delano Roosevelt (a Democrat) was president.

--The Korean War (30,000 military deaths) began when Harry S Truman (a Democrat) was president.

--The Vietnam War (50,000 military deaths) began when Lyndon Baines Johnson (a Democrat) was president.

In the space of a little less than 150 years, Democratic Party administrations have taken the United States into war at a cost of over 1 million American lives. And that's just counting deaths in our military. Add the deaths of enemy soldiers as well as civilian deaths, and the violence is indeed catastrophic. But should the United States, the country, be blamed or should the blame rest with the political party that takes America to war?

Again, back to the issue of perspective: When the Democratic Party is involved in the loss of life, the country of America takes the blame. That's historically evident in the perspective of the anti-war movement, and is still seen in the perspective of the Civil Rights movement. You will not hear of the work of the Democratic Party, George Wallace, Orval Faubus, or Lester Maddox in fighting against the Civil Rights movement. Rather you will hear of our American shame. It is America the country that is at fault. Just keep in mind that selectively casting blame toward a country or a political movement is an indoctrination technique, and the Democrat Party practices it well.

OK, so what's the harm of shading one's perspective to implicate Republicans for all things bad, and hold Democrats up as shining examples of purity? Nothing, really, except that a better job can be done. These feelings and beliefs can be firmly ingrained if the indoctrination starts at an early age.

That's why The Democrat Children's Movement would start in grade school with weekly assemblies and audio/visual presentations of the anti-Republican themes. The "Destroying the Environment" theme might appeal to the younger students, with the more social themes (harming children; stealing from our seniors; engaging in hate crimes) appealing to the middle grades. Themes associated with the Constitution and the economy would be presented in high school. The goal would be that upon graduation from secondary school, students would have an unquestioning belief in the negative qualities of Republicans. Our anti-Republican culture would be secure.

Doing a more effective job of teaching our anti-Republican culture: That's the job of the Democrat Children's Movement.

8
HUMAN RIGHTS COME TO AMERICA

Have you ever been surprised to read about the widespread human rights violations going on in America? The news usually comes from organizations like Amnesty International, or Human Rights Watch, but various countries around the world usually pick up the chant. China counters accusations of human rights violations within its own borders with charges that similar violations occur in the United States. America is characterized as being seriously flawed in many ways, including its judicial system and foreign policy.

It may not be possible to set up our foreign policy so as to avoid criticism from other countries, but we can do something about our court system.

The Democrat Party finds an obvious example of a flawed justice system in the high proportion of people in our prisons who have dark skin color. The argument is made that a higher proportion of people with dark skin color means there is clear discrimination in the way we adjudicate those accused of crimes. Luckily there is a solution to this problem.

THE HATE CRIMES INITIATIVE

A straightforward way of dealing with an excess number of people with dark skin color in our prisons is to change the way the court system works. We currently have laws that grant stiffer penalties to individuals if the crime committed was intended as a statement of racial or social hatred. This becomes a bit tricky on occasion, because it is difficult to conclusively determine an individual's state of mind during the commitment of a crime. It lends itself to emotional outcomes rather than objective outcomes in the judicial process, and sometimes justice is not served. Wouldn't it be more straightforward if justice were simply adjudicated based on skin color?

Let's take the guilt or innocence part of a trial. If the defendant has dark skin color, the rules would stay the same: a unanimous jury verdict to convict. However, if the defendant's skin color were white, a simple majority of the members of the jury would be sufficient to convict. That is a simple change, and it would go a long way toward tilting the scales of justice in favor of those with dark skin color. In short, it becomes easier to convict a white person.

Here's an interesting twist on the concept. There could be standard gradations in skin color, so that the people adjudicated under the simple majority system would have to have very white skin color, with darker skin tones being tried under more strict conviction requirements.

Can you imagine the acclamation of support we would get from the international community? It would clearly differentiate between those who feel we should follow the Constitution in interpreting our laws versus those who think we should follow a more international standard.

We could even make sentencing and the death penalty itself dependent on skin color, with only those having white skin color being subject to capital punishment, while those with darker skin color would have a maximum sentence of life in prison. We could start by cutting by half the maximum sentence for crimes committed by people with dark skin color, and changing the sentencing guidelines as we get more experience with what becomes the acceptable mix of skin color within our prisons.

The criminal justice system in the United States would become a model for a tolerant society with a strong regard for human rights. The international community might also convince us to change sentencing guidelines for women and perhaps make changes in the standards for guilt and innocence. All we have to do is modify the concept of equal protection under the law, and give preferences to those who should have them.

You are probably beginning to doubt my sanity at this point, but stay with me for just a moment longer. The idea that skin color is an important consideration when meting out justice is a basic principle of the Democrat Party. It follows the natural inclination of the Democrat Party to classify human beings by gender, race, and wealth. While there are other classifications that are in play, these are "The Big Three".

You have seen news stories that classify people in this manner. A headline might appear in this format: "Hurricane Hits Florida – Low Income People Suffer Most". Another headline might be, "Flooding in New Mexico Disproportionately Hurts Hispanics". The news reports we read on a daily basis often relate human suffering to one of the major classifications of human beings used by the Democrat Party.

While we've got a long-standing policy in America of "equal justice for all", the Democrat Party holds to the belief that its classifications of human beings require the application of special treatment. Here's where the Hate Crimes Initiative comes into play. In our legal system, the Democrat Party thinks the concept of "equal justice" needs a slanted playing field.

I've shown how we could change the rules for adjudication and punishment of crimes to take into account skin tones. That would handle the problems related to those people with lighter skin tones who might have "hate in their hearts". It would also take care of the people with darker skin tones who might be suffering the indignities of disenfranchisement. Rather than forcing a defense counsel to plead the extenuating circumstances to a jury, a judge could immediately set the rules for adjudication and punishment based on the appearance of the accused. The playing field would be tilted to achieve the philosophical goals of the Democrat Party.

The formula could also be extended to gender and wealth. Rules for trying rape cases could be modified based upon whether the accused rapist is male or female. You could then integrate skin tone into the decision, and perhaps throw in a differential of some type for wealth differences between the accused and the victim. Over time the bugs could be worked out, and the Democrat Party sense of fairness based on appearance standards could become the law of the land.

Consider the Hate Crimes Initiative just a beginning.

9

MISTAKES HAPPEN

The Hate Crimes Initiative helps quantify who deserves preferential legal treatment and under what circumstances. It provides a structure for a sliding scale of justice, based on skin tone. It also shows a path for adjustments to be made for factors such as gender and wealth. The natural arbiter of these issues of fairness would be the Democrat Party.

But what if the fairness of the system breaks down as a result of subsequent events? What if new evidence is brought to bear? What happens then?

Maybe you've read in the newspaper of the person who was caught up in a crime spree, but really didn't want to see anyone badly hurt or killed? How about the individual who makes a good-faith commitment to a cause and then finds that the commitment is too great a burden to bear? These situations make headlines, and the theme is typically something about an uncaring system trapping a victimized individual in a situation of incredible suffering. But there is hope! The Democratic Party has a solution.

THE PREFERENCES TRIBUNAL

There are three areas where the Democratic Party would provide preferential treatment: legal jeopardy, economic jeopardy, and commitment problems. Here we truly have something for everyone.

Let's take a case where an individual is on Death Row

for committing multiple murders. As fate would have it, the person becomes adept at writing children's books, and actually contributes to society in a positive way. The time comes when his execution date is near, and the Preferences Tribunal is asked to show clemency.

The power of the Tribunal is that it does not have to consider the victim's side of the issue. Only the individual requesting preferential treatment is analyzed, and only in terms of a single issue: "Is the individual deserving?"

This simplifies things quite a bit. When only one side of the assailant/victim incident is considered, the problems are immediately cut in half. Also, when considering the question of whether or not a person is deserving of Democratic Party charity, there are only feelings involved. The Preferences Tribunal looks at the inner feelings of the individual and decides if he or she is "deserving".

Think of all the cases where this applies with people in legal jeopardy. In Colorado, we had a case where an individual kept mum about the dangers posed by a cohort on the run, and a policeman ended up being killed. Even though the person was not the one who actually pulled the trigger, she ended up doing jail time as a result of her behavior. If this case were brought before the Tribunal, the judges would not need to consider her behavior in reaching their decision. Rather, if she is judged to be deserving, the charity of the Tribunal would be granted. The powers of the Tribunal would be similar to those of the President of the United States in granting Presidential Pardons.

What about the area of economic charity? I'll bet several instances come to mind. How about the individual who declares bankruptcy, and feels the consequences are too strict? Maybe the person who has fallen on hard times because of a medical emergency that was not covered by insurance? Each day, the news has candidates for the Preferences Tribunal. The Democratic Party could use funds from its Excess Wealth and Income Tax to cover the costs of making life easier for these disadvantaged individuals.

The Preferences Tribunal could also do work in the area

where an individual makes a commitment of one type or another, and then feels the need to break that commitment. The Tribunal has to be careful not to take up trivial cases here. A typical example is the individual who chooses to serve his or her country by joining the armed forces, but then finds it immoral, illegal, or unjust to support the mission of the armed services. The Preferences Tribunal could arrange for the individual to be released from his or her commitment, but it would have to be careful of the message it sends in this regard. The Tribunal would have to emphasize that it does not look at the issue from the perspective of the entity that received the commitment from the individual. Rather, it evaluates simply the issue of whether or not the individual is deserving of charity. The offended institution or the victim of the individual's failed commitment is not addressed.

Who would make up the membership of the Tribunal? While the Democratic Party would run the Tribunal, its membership doesn't have to come from within the Party. Rather, what is needed from each member is an exquisite sense of fairness. One candidate that comes to mind from recent history is former Supreme Court Justice Sandra Day O'Connor. She has retired from the Supreme Court, but her ability to render decisions that show a relativistic sense of justice based on changing social circumstances make her a logical candidate for the Preferences Tribunal.

The mission of the Preferences Tribunal is to Right our Wrongs and create a more compassionate society. It's interesting to note that when you look at the Preferences Tribunal and its quest for helping those individuals deserving of charity, you almost get a religious feel to the mission. Yes, we've got charity…redemption…deliverance. Does it almost seem as though religion is in the air?

10

THE DEMOCRATIC PARTY BECOMING A RELIGION

This is an interesting development. I do think the Democrat Party (note that lack of the "ic") has already made the transformation. It maintains an anti-Republican belief system that is extraordinary. Members of the Democrat Party consider me an affront to their sensibilities simply because I registered as a Republican at the age of 21. Similarly, the tenets of the Democrat Party require the active pursuit of income redistribution and societal re-engineering in America. Since I do not share those beliefs, my mere existence is an annoyance. I am a heathen.

But a religion needs a clear purpose, and the Democrat Party fulfills this requirement perfectly. It has a well-defined strategy with three key principles:

1) Ridicule Republicans.
2) Legitimize anti-Republican thought.
3) Stay on message.

The "message" is that there must be more Democrats. Elect them, hire them, appoint them, or convert them. America must have more Democrats in positions of power. The way to do this is to attack Republicans as individuals. Characterize Republicans as bad people, and use the themes of the Democratic Party to make examples of the bad traits of Republicans. Legitimize those issues that are patently anti-Republican. No matter how outlandish, support anti-

Republican positions and make them seem reasonable.

I imagine you need a clear example to bring all of this into focus. Let me relate an experience I had when I worked for the old telephone company, U S WEST. It has to do with trust.

I think the year was 1987, and I was in Englewood, Colorado. Upper management wanted a focus group to help them understand what was required to gain employee trust for their various initiatives. Several of us in middle management were selected for the focus group, and we engaged in a discussion on the subject.

I can remember thinking, "This really is a waste of time". But I kept an open mind, and when it was my turn to contribute I told them what I thought.

My understanding of trust is that it has to be earned, and that you earn it by doing two things: telling the truth and making good decisions. I used as an example a teenager being given the family car to drive for the first time. You wouldn't necessarily do that unless you believed your son or daughter would make good decisions and tell the truth. If they earn your trust, you give them the keys to the car.

I tell you this story to set the stage. Gaining trust is one thing, but losing trust is another. The senior management at U S WEST thought they could "sell" the idea of trust. I don't think that is possible. You have to gain trust through direct interaction with those whose trust you hope to win.

On the flip side, it is possible to learn to distrust someone without any personal interaction. You can lose trust in another person just by hearing about them.

Here's where the Democrat Party comes in. Expanding on the "Bad Republican" theme, the Democrat Party has waged a continuing campaign aimed at destroying trust in President George W. Bush, a Republican. The technique is not to directly convince people to distrust the President of the United States. Rather, the campaign is to depict the Republican President as a liar and a miserable failure. For good measure, the Democrat Party throws in a characterization of the President as a moron.

The President was portrayed as being guilty of mismanaging

relations with Congress, doing poorly in college, and failing in every one of his personal endeavors, from piloting airplanes to running a business. The accusations were passed around as examples of someone who didn't tell the truth and who couldn't make good decisions.

The campaign worked! Polls would address the issue with questions like this: "Who do you trust more, Republican leaders or Democrat leaders?" The more the Democrat Party portrayed the President as not telling the truth and not making good decisions, the more the public lost trust in him.

People in Canada even picked up on the campaign. Within the Canadian government, the Director of Communications for Prime Minister Jean Chretien made private comments about President Bush being a "moron", and it ended up costing her job. In 2002, she resigned over the controversy.

What does this have to do with Religion? It shows how repetitive accusations can be used to create a belief system. Whether or not you rationally think a person with a Harvard MBA is a moron, when you hear the accusation over and over, you come to believe it. Belief systems are what characterize religions, and the Democrat Party has a belief system that matches the themes of the Democratic Party. Once you come to believe the themes, you have embraced the religious component of the Democrat Party.

And why would you believe the themes? At the core is the issue of trust. I am reminded of this fact whenever I hear people in the Democrat Party use the expression, "We did all that we could do". Maybe it's a foreign policy issue or a domestic policy issue, but it's used in a context that makes you think of a physician that has just lost a patient. You don't tell the physician, "Let's wait for the After-Action Report!" Instead, you trust that the physician truly did everything that could be done to save the patient's life. It's this same level of trust that is given to the Democrat Party. When people in the Democrat Party make assertions, Americans trust them. It's based upon feelings, and it is a reflection of our anti-Republican culture.

There is another link between the Democrat Party and

religious feelings. It involves the issue of charity.

You might think of charity as being the sole province of religions. Helping the needy and giving relief to the poor are theological virtues. We automatically associate them with religions. But what if you are an organization trying to galvanize the emotions of the group that supports you, and that group has the inherent human desire to help others? Why not capitalize on these emotions? Define yourself as the group primarily responsible for bringing safety and comfort to the disadvantaged. Make it so that traditional faith-based initiatives are subordinate, even "improper" avenues for charity. Establish the Democrat Party as the one true path toward charity.

It is a stealth technique that is used to expand from the political to the religious realm, and it works extremely well. The Democrat Party has a "moral lock" on charity, and they wield it as a birthright. They define those who are deserving of charity and those who are not. They are the gatekeepers, and are literally in competition with their religious brethren to serve the needs of the poor. It is the Democrat Party that decides who within America is deserving of charity.

But let's not overlook the Democratic Party. Its transformation as a religion comes down to one determining factor. It is an emotional factor, and it may take you by surprise.

That factor is hate.

The Democratic Party is gradually becoming defined by its hate for the opposing party, and it is here that the line between religion and politics begins to blur. At times the religious aspect of the ideology leads, and at other times the political aspects are in the forefront. The link that holds the two together - the nexus - is hate.

The current head of the Democratic National Committee is delighted to be quoted as saying "I hate Republicans!" While that is a great rallying cry for the true believers, it is also an ideological turning point. Religions use hate to mobilize their followers. The more fanatical religions extoll hatred for the followers of other religious beliefs. Religions that are more moderate focus their hatred on abstractions. You might see hatred shown for the Devil, or for the control such an entity has over human temptations.

I know, I know. You're thinking, "When someone claims to hate Republicans, they really don't mean it." My only comment is that this is a bit like the initial reporting of a news event. Remember how we went through the idea of watching for the first reports? It is in these first reports that you see the theme being presented in the greatest relief. It is here that it is easy to see who is portrayed as wearing the black hats. Later on, the story will be modified or perhaps retracted. It is then that you will see the clarifying analysis or even the occasional "If I offended anyone with my words, I offer my sincere regrets..." type of apology. But keep in mind that if you want to see the heart of the issue (and catch the theme), watch the opening coverage. The same thing is true when you hear those initial "offhand remarks". They are the most revealing.

Anyway, when hatred is focused on a political party, you might expect there to be an emotional reaction. The fact that Americans exhibit no outrage at this type of speech is a measure of the intensity of our anti-Republican culture. Substitute another ideological group for the term "Republicans" and see if your emotions change. What does it say when you have an emotional reaction to the expression "I hate black people" or "I hate Jews" and yet you think it is no big deal when someone says "I hate Republicans"? Being racist or anti-Semitic is a bad thing. Being anti-Republican is not.

Continuing on, let's say the Democratic Party is well on its way to becoming a religion. What would be the major indications of such a transformation? It's possible our judicial system will show us the way. The American legal system will be our early-warning system.

You might be familiar with the concept of "jury nullification". Let me introduce you to the concept of "Democrat nullification". Here is an example:

Suppose there is a person somewhere in America who feels that someone who says "The British government has learned that Saddam Hussein recently sought significant quantities of uranium from Africa." is a truly bad person. Let's further assume the person with those feelings is a male, and is upset that less than half the American people feel as he does. To ease his frustration, he decides to bomb a building in the financial district of an American city.

He carries out the deed, ends up being caught and is prosecuted. (There are laws against this kind of activity.) At his trial, he uses as his defense the principle that he was simply fighting the Vast Right-Wing Conspiracy. He supports his claim with the example of a former President of the United States who justified lying under oath with the same reasoning. He points out that fighting the Vast Right-Wing Conspiracy is a "Badge of Honor".

He further enhances his defense by downplaying the suffering of those impacted by his act. Borrowing from the writings of a Professor at the University of Colorado, he characterizes those injured in the explosion as "little Eichmanns".

Luckily, he finds a sympathetic jury. This is the type of jury that sees a political dimension to justice. They would probably invoke the Patrick Fitzgerald treatment, (where an Independent Counsel characterizes lying under oath as a VERY serious issue) when the defendant is a Republican. But this jury finds a kinder, gentler treatment (where lying under oath is NOT a terribly serious issue) when the defendant is a Democrat. Our hypothetical perpetrator has the good fortune to be a member of the Democratic Party.

Even though the prosecution is thorough in presenting evidence of the alleged crime, the jury is not swayed. It acquits the defendant, and sends a message to the American people that "the end justifies the means". The belief that you are fighting the Vast Right-Wing Conspiracy becomes a legitimate justification for performing illegal acts. Fighting the Vast Right-Wing Conspiracy trumps the Rule of Law!

I think we are being subtly prepared for the legitimacy of this type of legal behavior. If you watch game shows on television (where a set of judges evaluate a contestant but the television audience gets to call in their votes) you see the principle in practice. The people with the necessary credentials to decide the issue (the judges) sometimes get trumped by the viewing audience. If a contestant would be the winner based upon skill and competence, but ends up being a loser because another contestant is more popular with the viewing audience, you get a feel for the concept of Democrat nullification.

Those of you who were around to witness the verdict in the O. J. Simpson case certainly have an idea of what is meant by jury nullification. The idea of Democrat nullification seems far-fetched, but I wouldn't be surprised to see an instance of it within the next decade or two. I think the most promising area where it might garner support would be in the trial of an "Eco-terrorist" who is accused of something like arson or destruction of property. The radical environmentalist movement is one that is governed by passion and a sense of supremacy of the ideals of the movement, perhaps more so than other groups within the Democratic Party. When a person's political ideals become supreme to cultural influences such as nationality or family, the political ideology of the person tends to cross over into the arena of religion.

Supremacy of ideology is being tested by the Democratic Party on a daily basis. You see it in the battles against the influence of the "Religious Right" or the "Fundies" (religious fundamentalists). Here in Colorado, the Catholic Church got into the battle by holding a pro-life stance against the Democratic Party's issue of abortion rights.

It might seem a trivial sort of thing, but it goes to the core value of the Democratic Party: fighting for supremacy of ideology. If you are a Democrat, you must believe in Democratic Party principles. If you are a Democrat and a Catholic, you must choose which ideology is supreme: your religion or your politics. Here in Denver, Archbishop Charles J. Chaput, head of the Roman Catholic Archdiocese, put his foot down. It was 2004, and Senator John Kerry was the Democratic Party candidate for President. Senator Kerry happened to be Catholic, and advanced the notion that believing in a woman's right to choose and being a Catholic were not incompatible ideas. Archbishop Chaput went on record as saying that if you were a Catholic, this was not the case. You were obligated to be against abortion.

He was immediately attacked by the Democratic Party. His sin was characterized as being that he had not maintaining neutrality in the arena of politics. However, his true transgression was that he held that religious ideology trumped political ideology. This was political blasphemy!

I got the feeling that the Catholic Church was a bit befuddled by being labeled a part of the Religious Right. The Church doesn't move very quickly in changing dogma, and was simply stating a long-held tenet. I also don't think that the Catholic Church perceives the Democratic Party as a religious threat. Unfortunately, the feeling is not mutual.

While the fight for supremacy of ideology is a characteristic of religions, and the Democratic Party is certainly "in the fight", there are other indicators of how the Democratic Party is moving toward becoming a religion. Let's take a look at the operation of the Air America Radio network.

This is a network of radio stations in America that cater to the political thought of the Democratic Party. You will hear commentary by people dedicated to the ideology of the Democratic Party, and you will hear it non-stop throughout the day. The format of the commentary is what is striking about the network. It virtually mimics the format of the Christian Broadcast Network. The CBN shows are dedicated to the Christian faith, and continually showcase themes of Christianity. A particular show might feature a monologue highlighting a current event, a follow-up analysis of the event in a conversational format, and then a summarization of the impact of the event on a particular religious theme.

Air America Radio uses almost the same playbook. It covers the news, but with a slant toward the themes of the Democratic Party. The Al Franken Show might just as well be titled "The Ministry of Al Franken". The Randi Rhodes Show could be called "The Randi Rhodes Devotional". There is a recurring sameness to the programs.

The shows will start with a monologue that highlights the Democratic Party theme of the day (Republicans are Bad People, Republicans are Destroying the Environment, Republicans are Shredding the Constitution, Republicans are Turning the Economy into a Catastrophe, etc.). A featured guest will give witness to the crooked dealings of the Republicans with first-person accounts. Call-in participants will then give testimonials confirming similar experiences and revelations. The host will link the personal anecdotes, and give context to them by relating them to the particular theme of the day.

Not sure what the "theme of the day" might be? Here are some examples that come to mind:

--Republicans bow to corporate interests instead of the interests of the American people.
--Republicans support wars based on lies.
--Republicans suppress free speech.
--Republicans want to turn America into a theocracy.
--Republicans encourage torture against enemy combatants.
--Republicans advocate the death penalty for abortion doctors.
--Republicans blame the media for the ethical problems of Republicans.
--Republicans preach the sanctity of marriage while embracing high divorce rates.
--Republicans discriminate against people who are gay.
--Republicans embrace domestic spying.
--and so on...

Does it feel like a religious experience to listen to Air America Radio? That is a personal perception. But one thing is certain: The broadcast techniques employed are the same as those used by traditional religious organizations. The parallels are stunning.

There is one final dimension of the Democratic Party that has strong religious tones. It is the role of activists.

I think most people have a positive connotation for the

term "activist". People who are passionate about their beliefs deserve a certain amount of respect. But what if you made a small substitution in the terminology? What if instead of "Democratic Party Activists", the term were "Democratic Party Evangelicals"?

Once again, the parallels can be striking. In religious circles, you think of people who are disciples, spreading the teachings of their religion. You've got young people going on missions and immersing themselves in religious thought. Can the same thing be happening within the Democratic Party? If you are a Democratic Party activist, does it feel like a religious mission to go to a Republican gathering and try to disrupt it? Does it give one a sense of pursuing a higher calling? In what ways are the feelings different?

I think religion and the Democratic Party become intertwined based on strength of belief. Former President Jimmy Carter makes a distinction in religious groups between "fundamentalists" and "evangelicals". The evangelicals are OK; they are just doing their thing. The fundamentalists are the ones wearing the black hats. They have two bad traits:

1) They think they (and they alone) are right.
2) They feel that they don't make mistakes.

His contention is that religious groups with this type of philosophy gravitate toward the Republican Party, and their influence is doing damage to America.

He certainly may have a point, but I wonder if he has considered whether the fundamentalist traits he lists are in any way applicable to the Democratic Party? The emphasis the Democratic Party puts on battling religion and religious groups consumes a lot of energy. Why the obsession with combating religion? Consider these questions:

-- If you believe in the right to an abortion as the primary component of your ideology, does that become your "God"? Does the Christian religious construct of "The Father, The Son, and The Holy Ghost" not have a rhythmic similarity to the words "Pro-Choice, Abortion, and A Woman's Right to

Choose"?
-- Do the Reverend Al Sharpton and the Reverend Jesse Jackson devote as much of their time to the practice of religion as to the practice of their politics?
-- Is Allegiance the core issue? When you define yourself as a member of the Democratic Party, is there an implicit assumption of the supremacy of your political beliefs? Does being a Democrat trump the calling of your religion, race, ethnicity, work affiliation, family, and even your country?

There is a long tradition of separation of church and state in America. If the Democratic Party is a religion, then it risks major philosophical and legal challenges. It also must be careful as it tries to divide Catholics based on their abortion ideology. The challenge is to acquire religious fervor in the devotion of its followers, but not to antagonize people of strong religious faith.

The melding of religion and politics truly becomes a potent force. We see it in the Middle East and other parts of the world. If your political figures are all from the same religion, the society and culture of the country are easily manipulated. It's a path we've avoided so far in America, but it doesn't hurt to keep our eyes open and be watchful as we head into the future.

11

SOME FINAL THOUGHTS

Religion and politics can be caustic. I know of several families that say they can't discuss these two subjects while at the dinner table. If you want to be a family that CAN discuss politics and religion over dinner, just make it a rule that nobody can leave the table if they are going to leave "mad". Everyone has to resolve their angry feelings and make the necessary apologies before leaving.

There is power in creating religious intensity in politics. It elevates ideology, justifies sacrifice, and motivates people to give of their time and money. I think deep down, everyone realizes that this is powerful stuff. But in America, mixing religion and politics is generally understood to be a bad thing. We have separation of church and state written into our Constitution. Our founding fathers had firsthand experience that told them Theocracy was not the way to go. That's why a political party becoming a religion has to be a stealth action. I don't think anyone in the Democratic Party would acknowledge that the Party is moving in that direction.

To really understand what is happening to the Democratic Party, you have to approach it from the perspective of an atheist. If you start by denying the concept of a supreme being, then what are the attributes that make up a religion? What common characteristics define Christians, Muslims, Hindus, etc.? When you start looking at the ways these groups deal with good and evil, conduct their ceremonies, and motivate their followers, you start to see the parallels.

There is not one religion that believes other religions are on the right path to salvation. It is just a question of whether or not to tolerate those other religions. The Democratic Party does not intend to tolerate other political parties. After all, it is these political groups that stand between it and the widespread adoption of its political thought. If the Democratic Party can obtain political supremacy, it can dictate the policies of social engineering and redistribution of wealth that define its mission. That's why it is interesting to visualize the Democratic Party as a force gaining control of certain institutions within our society: so that we can attempt to understand the practical results of its ideology.

Wouldn't it be fun to see these institutions in action? The White Male Draft would engineer a society that has exactly the right proportion of ethnic and racial groups. The Excess Wealth and Income Tax would get just the right income mix throughout our society. Our criminal justice system would be fine-tuned with the application of the Hate Crimes Initiative. Young people would develop the correct attitude and perspective with the Democrat Children's Movement. Any minor problem areas would be resolved with the Preferences Tribunal. All we need to do is give the Democratic Party the power it needs, and it will take care of us.

Will we be better off? The implication of having our society structured properly is that there has to be an ultimate authority in charge that makes these "correct" decisions. What if the Democratic Party, in its quest to make things look right, doesn't actually make each of us happy? Maybe a more interesting question is, "Will control of American society be enough?"

There is allure in the concept of a perfect society. It's just a question of who gets to define what is "perfect". In the meantime, there's a group that wants your allegiance.

They will make you popular.

They will get you more than the other guy.

They will sign you up today.